Incest and Sexuality

A Guide to Understanding and Healing

Wendy Maltz
Beverly Holman

Lexington Books
D.C. Heath and Company/Lexington, Massachusetts/Toronto

D0628598

Library of Congress Cataloging-in-Publication Data

Maltz, Wendy.
  Incest and sexuality.

  Bibliography: p.
  Includes index.
  1. Incest victims—Sexual behavior. 2. Incest
victims—Mental health. 3. Incest victims—Family
relationships. 4. Sex therapy. I. Holman, Beverly.
II. Title [DNLM: 1. Child Abuse—popular works.
2. Incest-popular works. 3. Sex Behavior—popular
works. 4. Sex Offences—popular works. WA 320 M2625i]
RC560.153M35   1987   616.85'83   86–45635
ISBN 0–669–14083–X (alk. paper)
ISBN 0–669–14085–6 (pbk. : alk. paper)

Published simultaneously in Canada
Printed in the United States of America
Casebound International Standard Book Number: 0–669–14083–X
Paperbound International Standard Book Number: 0–669–14085–6
Library of Congress Catalog Card Number: 86–45635

The paper used in this publication meets the minimum requirements of
American National Standard for Information Sciences—Permanence of
Paper for Printed Library Materials, ANSI Z39.48–1984. ∞™

90 91 18 17 16 15 14

Contents

Preface

For the past year and a half we have worked jointly to produce this book. Initially we planned to do a research study and from that write a pamphlet for incest survivors and their partners about dealing with the sexual aftereffects of incest. But as time went on, we expanded our existing materials and realized that we had the ingredients for a book. We each put in many long, hard hours of research, writing, editing, and general production. Before we began, our lives were already filled with family and work commitments. It was often very difficult to keep focusing our energies on the book. Constant exposure to the painful details of sexual abuse left us feeling emotionally sensitive at times.

However, the effort was not without its rewards. We were inspired by the strengths and abilities of survivors to overcome their childhood traumas. We were provided with opportunities to expand our existing knowledge and expertise in treating incest survivors. We gained new appreciation for the art and discipline of expressing thoughts on paper.

Our contributions to the book were different and yet complementary. The original idea for writing on the subject of incest and sexuality came from Wendy. Five years ago, she and another Eugene, Oregon, incest therapist, Sandy Solomon, met with teen survivors to gather more information for a statewide counselor training workshop on incest and teen sexuality. Some of the ideas and theoretical models in our book had their beginnings in materials developed for that workshop. The teen incest survivor interviews contained in the book are from transcripts of those early group sessions.

Wendy proposed the research and writing project to Beverly in the summer of 1984. At that time Beverly was facilitating adult incest survivor therapy groups at a mental health clinic and was attending graduate school at the University of Oregon in Counseling Psychology. She conducted an extensive review of existing literature on the interface of incest and sexuality. She administered a questionnaire to thirty-five survivors who were in incest treatment groups. Beverly analyzed the results and wrote a thesis entitled "The Sexual Impact of Incest on Adult Women." Much of our book is based on materials gathered from the literature review, research, and questionnaire responses.

In January 1985, we began writing the book. Wendy wrote the bulk of the initial draft; together we rewrote and edited subsequent drafts. While she was working on the book, Beverly graduated and continued to counsel incest survivors in her private practice and at local mental health clinics. Her background in incest resolution therapy and family therapy has contributed an important clinical perspective to the book. Simultaneously, Wendy's private practice grew in the number of incest survivors and partners who wanted help in overcoming the sexual difficulties they were experiencing. From this clinical work and from workshops she had presented on sexuality, Wendy developed models and strategies specifically for sex therapy with incest survivors. She interviewed survivors and partners to obtain their stories for the book. The names in these accounts have been changed to ensure confidentiality. Many of the guidelines, interventions, and analogies in the book are Wendy's original contributions. Beverly assumed the administrative task of preparing the final manuscript.

Acknowledgments are due to many people. Steve Schweitzer, Ph.D., provided academic consultation for the research at the University of Oregon. Thoughtful assistance in editing and content was provided by Sandy Solomon, M.S.W.; Nancy Evergreen, M.A.; Judith Engle, Ph.D.; Mary Ann Huyser, M.A.; Marty Acker, Ph.D.; and Bee Sholes, M.A. Members of the Lane County, Oregon, Incest Clinicians's Group assisted in administering the questionnaire for our study and provided enthusiastic support. In particular, we thank Carolyn Rexius; Gail Wiemann; Mary Hinman, M.S.; Jill Wolf, M.S.; Norma Sue Webster; Margie Templeton, M.A.; Dorothy Abelson, M.S.W.; and Diane Maria. We appreciate the information, materials, and consultation provided by Doug Ricks, Peter Elliot-Wotton, and John Preble, M.S.W., on sexuality concerns of male incest survivors. We thank Dianne Watson, M.A., our colleague and friend, for helping us stay focused and for helping to keep the ball rolling to the finish line. Thanks are also due to Barbara Land for her careful work in typing the manuscript.

A special thanks goes to our husbands, Larry Maltz and Sabin Lamson, whose support made it possible for us to carve out the time and energy for this project. We are grateful for their love and affection, which keep us mindful of how nurturing intimate relationships can be. We also thank our children, Jules and Cara Maltz, Jesse Kocher, and Emilie Lamson, for patiently allowing our endless absences.

Most of all, we want to thank the incest survivors whom we have come to know and care about in our work as therapists and researchers. Their openness in exploring and sharing the intimate aspects of their lives made this book possible. We dedicate this book to them and to all survivors of child sexual abuse. We hope they will find it helpful in their journey.

Introduction

This book has been written for survivors of incest who want to explore both how the sexual abuse may have affected their sexuality and what they can do about it. Intimate partners of survivors and therapists who have clients who are survivors may also find this book useful in developing a supportive and understanding approach to sexual concerns. Special sections have been written with partners and therapists in mind. We have chosen to use the term "survivor" instead of "victim" because it better communicates the ability people have to recover from abuse.

This book has been written from the perspective of female incest survivors because most incest survivors are female, current research has focused almost exclusively on females, and our contact has primarily been with female survivors. However, a male perspective is important and we have consequently devoted an appendix to addressing sexuality concerns of male survivors [See Appendix A]. We believe that male survivors as well as female survivors of types of sexual abuse other than those we have discussed will find useful information in this book. We hope they will be able to adapt the content and treatment approaches to their own situations.

Sexuality is a very sensitive and emotionally charged subject for incest survivors. Confronting the graphic details of sexual abuse can be a shocking experience. Therefore, we recommend that people reading this book have a support system, such as a friend or counselor, with whom they can discuss any feelings that may arise. We also suggest that readers give themselves permission to skip over any graphic descriptions contained in the book and to stop and take a break from the reading when needed. We suggest that readers use the parts of the book they find helpful and not put expectations on themselves to address the topic in any particular way or move through the subject matter faster than is comfortable. Our goal has been to create a framework for understanding so that sexual concerns can be addressed in a relaxed and positive manner.

Survivors of sexual abuse are definitely not alone. Estimates vary, and because of the high number of unreported cases, solid data is not available. However, studies show that a range of 9 to 52 percent of adult women and 3 to 9 percent of adult men report having been sexually abused as children by either family members or strangers.[1] The figures are much higher when the definition of sexual abuse is broadened to include experiences such as being forced or encouraged to watch sexual activity or being forced to stimulate oneself in front of another person.

When we permit the inclusion of more common experiences that contain elements of sexual abuse, such as receiving obscene phone calls, being called sexually derogatory names, and being treated as a sexual object, it becomes evident that almost all females and many males have experienced some form of sexual abuse.

In many ways, our American culture fosters the existence of abusive elements in sexual relationships. During the developmental years, males and females are taught stereotyped sex roles that set the stage for how sexual activity should take place. Males are often taught that being unfeeling, uncommunicative, and sexually demanding is part of being masculine. Teen boys express this attitude in such statements as "If I don't press for sex with her, she might be angry or think I'm gay," and "Even if she says no, maybe she still wants it and expects it from me." Sexual activities become an opportunity to gain peer status and show conquering abilities rather than to relate meaningfully to another person.

Teen females are culturally socialized to seek approval from others by being passive, adaptive, and physically attractive. They are taught to downplay their intelligence and assertiveness for fear of being seen as unfeminine. The message is that females should be responsive to males' sexual needs. Paradoxically, females are also inaccurately viewed as having ultimate responsibility for whatever sexual activity takes place. Sex is often engaged in as a means of maintaining the status of having a boyfriend or with the hope of securing future commitments. Thus girls learn to exploit themselves sexually toward a nonsexual goal. Little cultural recognition is given to the healthy expression of female sexual feelings. Instead, sexual directness in young women is considered socially out of place.

The American media portray sex as a casual activity, unplanned, with no mention of birth control, the prevention of sexually transmitted disease, or emotional responsibility to a partner. Many times sex is portrayed as a way to exert control and power over another person. Television, movies, and books teach Americans to use sex for secondary gain. Blatant examples are the teen slash films, in which sex is associated with violence. These films often show rape scenes that have no apparent connection to the plot, and women who respond positively to aggressive acts against them. Much adult pornography continues the sex stereotyping by portraying women as content to be sex toys for men's pleasure.

It appears that our society has been training boys to be sexually exploitive, and girls to be sexually victimized, without full awareness of how this has been happening or of the unpleasant repercussions it implies for both sexes. As adults, many men feel ashamed when they recall the times they pressured a girl into sex. What they most desperately wanted was to be really loved and accepted. They thought sex was a means to that end and lacked other skills to develop intimacy.

The high rate of sexual abuse in our culture dramatically underlines the strong need for sex to be taught and portrayed in a different way. Whether it is engaged in alone or with a partner, sex is a physical activity that is based on a natural biological drive. The circumstances surrounding sexual activity determine whether it is positive or negative. It would be very beneficial to our culture if we were to begin teaching sexual relating as a serious activity that can be approached with personal integrity, a willingness to assume responsibility, and an ability to delay gratification. Were sexual activity to be undertaken responsibly, with accurate information and healthy sex role models, the negative repercussions could be reduced.

Sexual abuse has finally been recognized as a major problem in our society. Public awareness and education about childhood sexual abuse has mushroomed in the past five years. The public reaction to incest has changed from one of disbelief to one of active concern. Current and former victims of abuse have been coming out of their hidden worlds of pain to get help. Hotlines, treatment programs, and reading materials are now available and in demand.

Incest is the most common form of child sexual abuse. We define incest as any sexual contact between a child or adolescent and a person who is closely related or perceived to be related, including stepparents and live-in partners of parents. Most victims are female; most perpetrators are male. In the majority of cases it is a father or stepfather who abuses a child. Incest also includes sexual activity initiated by siblings, cousins, mothers, uncles, aunts, or grandparents. Incest involves sexual activity that occurs only once as well as activity that takes place over an extended period of time, often several years. The types of sexual activity include fondling, oral sex, anal sex, and intercourse. The breakdown of trust within the family heightens the psychological damage caused by the sexual abuse.

Many women (estimates run as high as 50 percent) do not remember their incestuous experiences until something triggers the memory in adulthood. Those women who do remember may be disappointed to find that the important steps of remembering the incest and disclosing it to others do not bring automatic relief from the legacy of pain and problems the incest has left behind. Understanding why one has always felt shy undressing in front of others does not make the shyness go away. Likewise, addressing other issues such as anger and grief, while crucial to the work of incest, does not necessarily result in resolution of sexual concerns.

Based on our clinical work and research, we believe that a person's sexuality is significantly affected by the experience of childhood sexual abuse. Sexuality involves attitudes, feelings, and behavior concerning sexual activity. It reflects one's gender identity (male or female), the types of sexual expression pursued, and sexual preference (heterosexual, homosexual, or bisexual). Societal messages and sexual interactions early in life strongly influence the development of adult sexual attitudes, behaviors, and identity.

Most incest survivors have some sexual issues. Some women have extensive concerns about sexual relating and others have minor ones. Experiencing incest is only one source of sexual concerns. Many women who are not incest survivors also have sexual problems. Sources of sexual problems for both survivors and those who have not experienced incest can be medical conditions, inadequate knowledge, lack of experience, sexually repressive childhoods and poor relationship dynamics.

Many benefits can be derived from addressing the relationship between incest and sexuality. As a society, we can become more informed about the real damage that occurs. Our motivation to combat sexual abuse can be strengthened. Parents can recognize signs of abuse earlier and take a more active, outspoken role in protecting their children. Sexual offenders can be directly challenged when they deny or try to excuse the effects of sexual abuse with statements like "She was too young to know what was happening"; "She was asleep and probably forgot it"; and "I did it for her benefit." These remarks are absurd when contrasted with the enormous pain survivors experience and the difficult process recovery requires. And for adult survivors of incest, studying the relationship between incest and sexuality can answer questions they may have about what they are feeling and how they are behaving sexually. Survivors can gain knowledge and skills that will enable them to resolve their sexual issues.

1
Sexuality: Why Bother?

Incest survivors want to resolve the issue of sexuality, yet they
don't want to go near it.
   —Nancy Evergreen, M.A., Incest Treatment Specialist

To women who have been sexually abused, talking about sex or
even thinking about sex can be emotionally upsetting. For
many survivors, sexuality has become confused with sexual
abuse, even though intellectually they understand there is a difference.
They may find it difficult to imagine positive, healthy, enjoyable sexual activity. Sexual activity has generally become associated with emotional and physical pain. Justifiably, a survivor may wonder why she
should bother exploring her sexuality.

She may not want to bother. Some survivors are not ready to look
at sexuality issues. If and when to address sexuality is an individual
decision and should not be forced; survivors have experienced too
much force in sexual areas already. One woman who had been repeatedly sexually molested in her teens by both her stepfather and grandfather explained, "Sex is the last priority for me. Enjoying an orgasm is
a ridiculous goal when I'm trying to stop drinking and being self-
destructive." It's not a good time to look into sexuality concerns if a
survivor doesn't have a basic feeling of worth about herself, if she is
concerned for her safety or survival, or if she lacks the interest and
motivation to explore this area.

Though dissatisfaction may exist in their current relationships,
some survivors prefer to avoid addressing their sexual concerns. The
idea of making sexual changes is perceived as threatening. Opening
themselves to the possibility of sexual pleasure can be extremely difficult for survivors. They do not want to feel sexually vulnerable again.
They may not want to believe sexual pleasure is possible. There is a
great fear of failure. One woman said, "If positive sexuality is my right
. . . I don't think I want that right!" She saw having sex with her hus-

band as something she did as a duty in order to keep things calm. She confided that she hated the sexual experiences but had taught herself to "grin and bear it" for his sake. The situation had grown "acceptable." She feared her husband's reaction if she were to be honest with him.

Yet there are many survivors who feel ready to develop their sexuality in a positive way. For them, it is worth the time and energy necessary to explore their sexuality because of their strong desire to experience sexual pleasure and contentment. Usually this desire surfaces in the later stages of incest therapy, when self-esteem is higher and women are able to feel their strength and power. There may be a desire to reclaim what was taken from them by the offenders—their sexual innocence. As one woman shared, "I want to feel good about sex. It's my way of totally breaking my father's hold over me. I don't want what he did to get in the way of my sexual enjoyment with a future partner." Having a partner whom she loves and feels fully loved by can be a tremendous motivator for a survivor to overcome sexual problems that resulted from early abuse.

Teens are another population of incest survivors who are often motivated to address sexuality concerns. Usually they are very curious about sexuality and are eager to develop healthier sexual attitudes, since they have not experienced repetitive abusive patterns as adults. This can be an excellent time for them to resolve confusions and fears about sex. To prevent future sexual problems, time can be spent in teen incest treatment programs focusing on common sexual concerns and the sexual repercussions of incest.

Sexuality refers to how people feel about their bodies and genitals, how they choose to express sexual energy, and how and with whom they prefer to share sexual feelings. In sexual expression, a woman projects her intimate self outward. She takes hidden aspects of herself—her genitals and their sensations—and reveals them to herself and perhaps to a partner. When this is done in the context of healthy, positive sexual expression, the experience can be extremely satisfying. On a physical level, individuals can experience pleasurable sensations and tension release, which then reinforce good feelings about the body. On a social level, healthy sexual expression involves intimacy and an exchange of feelings of positive regard and acceptance. Thus, healthy sexuality can greatly enhance one's sense of self-esteem.

All women have a right to positive, healthy sexuality. Incest survivors, having this right, can redefine sexuality for themselves and develop ways of relating sexually with others that feel good to them. To ensure against further abuse and to create healthy, positive sexual experiences, survivors must make sure certain basic conditions are met. Though these conditions may vary somewhat from person to person, the five that follow (called CERTS) seem essential.

CERTS for Positive, Healthy Sexuality

1. *Consent:* I can freely and comfortably choose whether or not to engage in sexual activity. I am able to stop the activity at any time during the sexual contact.

2. *Equality:* My feeling of personal power is on an equal level with my partner. Neither of us dominates the other.

3. *Respect:* I have a positive regard for myself and for my partner. I feel respected by my partner. I feel supportive of my partner and supported by my partner.

4. *Trust:* I trust my partner on both a physical and emotional level. We have a mutual acceptance of vulnerability and an ability to respond to it with sensitivity.

5. *Safety:* I feel secure and safe within the sexual setting. I am comfortable with and assertive about where, when and how the sexual activity takes place. I feel safe from the possibility of unwanted pregnancy and/or sexually transmitted diseases.

When these conditions are met, sexual activity can become fun, nurturing, and a true expression of caring. It's a natural human response to want to be physically close to people who one cares for, to share love and appreciation with a hug, handshake or kiss. With an intimate partner, under circumstances of mutual respect and consent, this caring can be expressed further with touch involving sensitive, private parts of the body. Each person sharing sexually can feel in control. The couple focuses on feeling emotionally at ease and close, not on one person getting something from the other. Defining sexual expression in the context of *nurturing, healing closeness* can help survivors to consider claiming sexuality as something beneficial for themselves. Experiencing sex when one's body, mind, and emotions are united in pleasurable desire is something totally different from being sexually abused—and definitely worth the effort it takes to overcome the sexual traumas from the abuse.

2
The Exploitation of Children

GIRL 1: He used to stick his penis in my bottom. He'd have
this stuff on it so it would slide. . . . He'd make me
stand over the counter and I'd tell him it hurted so
bad and he'd say, "Here, bite on this wash rag" or
something. It was just terrible. When he'd sodomize
me he'd be on the waterbed and I'd be down like
that, he'd have his hands on the back of my head . . .
so I couldn't really pull away to breathe.

GIRL 2: I'd bite him!

GIRL 1: When he's about two hundred pounds heavier than
you, you can't bite him or tell him no. He'd say it's
all in your head that you don't like it. . . . If you'd
just change your attitude . . . it's your attitude that's
bad. You've got the wrong attitude! And I'm sitting
there thinking, My attitude! You shouldn't even be
doing this!
                              —Excerpt from Teen Group

Incest lacks all the essential conditions for positive, healthy sexuality. There is no true consent, equality, respect, trust, or safety. Incest perpetrators use their victim's age, dependence, and immaturity to their advantage. They selfishly exploit the innocence of their victims.

Incest can include a wide range of sexual activities, from fondling to overt acts of intercourse and sodomy. While incest can be limited to one instance, it most often takes place repeatedly over time. Many survivors report frequent abuse that went on for a number of years and sometimes involved more than one perpetrator. Though experiences vary in intensity and duration, each woman's experience is valid and important, and deserves attention.

Because incest is universally regarded as wrong and harmful, practically all cultures have laws that forbid it. Incest is considered a deviant type of sexual behavior that warrants labeling the perpetrator a social criminal in need of behavioral restraint. Societies strive to protect children and adolescents from the physical and emotional harm that sexual abuse can cause. Most people realize that nonconsenting sexual behavior, which is present in incest, can be seriously damaging to the victim.

While in general societies legally recognize the premise that children are *never* capable of giving consent to an adult, perpetrators and sometimes survivors may have difficulty believing that this is so. In an unconscious attempt to justify their behavior and to minimize their responsibility, some perpetrators fool themselves into viewing the child as consenting. They may communicate this idea to the victim, who is then led to doubt her own perception of her role in the incest. Many survivors blame themselves for not having stopped the incest. They are afraid that they allowed it to occur and thus must assume responsibility for it. Some survivors enjoyed the physical sensations and closeness. Some survivors willingly participated in order to get the affection and attention of a loved adult or older child. However, these situations *do not* demonstrate consent. A child's relationship with a parent or close relative is too encumbered by physical and psychological dependency to ever include the possibility of free consent. When a power imbalance exists because of differences in age and sexual sophistication, real consent cannot exist.

David Finkelhor argues that children are unable to consent to sex because they are uninformed in every way about sex:

> Can children give informed consent to sex with adults? It is fairly evident they cannot. For one thing, children lack the information that is necessary to make an "informed" decision about the matter. They are ignorant about sex and sexual relationships. It is not only that they may be unfamiliar with the mechanics of sex and reproduction. More importantly they are generally unaware of the social meanings of sexuality. For example, they are unlikely to be aware of the rules and regulations surrounding sexual intimacy, and what it is supposed to signify. They are probably uninformed and inexperienced about what criteria to use in judging the acceptability of a sexual partner. They probably do not know much about the "natural history" of sexual relationships, what course they will take. And, finally, they have little way of knowing how other people are likely to react to the experience they are about to undertake, what likely consequences it will have for them in the future.[2]

The sexual contact demanded of children in incest involves strange sensations, sights, smells, and sounds, which children are unprepared for and often overwhelmed by. Survivors often remember how scary it was to witness their usually controlled fathers, uncles, or cousins become naked, erect, and hungry for secretive physical contact with them. Most survivors knew something was wrong with the contact but lacked the maturity needed to identify what was wrong and to express it. Here a survivor describes her frustration with communication limitations:

> I had no vocabulary to express my confusion, my fears, my view. A child has no vocabulary power, so adults rape children thinking the children don't know what's happening. Children *do know* — but children have no language . . . to communicate. It's like *being a prisoner in a foreign country,* and not knowing the language. . . . I cried a lot. I acted out a lot. I still have a problem with thought and verbal expression regarding sexual intercourse.

Children do not have a sufficiently strong sense of themselves or a clear enough understanding of others to fully realize what is happening and to assert their own best interests. It is usually not until they are in their late teens that people can even attempt to consent in a mature way to sexual activity. Before that time, they are extremely vulnerable to being fooled and exploited by others more sexually experienced than they are.

Children have a tendency to feel guilty for engaging in activities which they sense are wrong or bad, whether or not they have any control over their involvement. Perpetrators often play upon this tendency, using the guilt to gain more leverage over the victim. Such an experience is described by a survivor in the following story:

> I was molested by the next-door neighbor. I guess that I was between the ages of four and five when it first started. He — an older, fat, ugly man — had me do various sexual activities with him. This went on for several years, until I was about seven years old. I was afraid of this person and I hated the acts. I knew what I was doing was wrong, and I was afraid of being caught or my mother finding out. I felt tremendous shame and guilt. There were times when my mother suspected something was going on and confronted me about it, but I always denied the fact and felt even more guilt. I was afraid that my mother would think I was a horrible person if she ever found out. The neighbor always gave me candy after he was finished, which I always hid. I suppose that's why my mother started suspecting things. She found a lot of stale candy in bizarre places.

Finally my burden became too great, so I confided in one of my older cousins, who spent a lot of time at our house. He was about five or six years older than me, and for some reason I trusted him. That was a great mistake! I don't remember if it was right after I told him or sometime later when he used this information against me. I think I was about six when he blackmailed me. He told me that if I didn't have sex with him, he would tell my parents about the next-door neighbor molesting me. So I let him do with me what he wanted. I felt I had no other choice. I was scared of getting caught. The pain of intercourse was tremendous. I was also afraid I was going to get pregnant. I was old enough to know how people get pregnant, but I didn't know that I wasn't old enough to get pregnant. My cousin also burned me with a match in my private parts, trying to see what I looked like. I hated him, and still do.

Children need to feel that their initial sexual sensations are under their own control and for their own benefit. Self-exploration and self-stimulation create healthy early sexual experiences because they are motivated by the child's own desires, are engaged in privately, and occur in a relaxed setting. In contrast, children's sexual activities in incest are dominated by the perpetrator's emotional needs and selfish orientation toward sexuality. Tension, fear, betrayal, pain, and mistrust color the victim's sexual awakening. Thus, children are robbed of the opportunities to experience their sexuality as something that is primarily for themselves.

3
Family Influences

Incest survivors grow up in families that often appear to be like any other family. However, a closer look reveals primary relationships that are riddled with secrets and psychological stress. Like a team of rock climbers connected by ropes that scale the side of a mountain, all family members are integrally connected in a journey through time. A family "team" operates in a state of interdependence, with younger members extremely dependent on the older members for guidance and support. The inappropriate behavior of any one member has consequences for all the other members and seriously jeopardizes the integrity of the family team as a whole. An undetected abusive relationship between two members of the family creates layers of dishonesty that extract a personal toll on those maintaining the secret and that weaken the whole team's ability to function. Trust is betrayed when forced secretiveness prevails.

Understanding family influences can benefit survivors. They can learn how each member of their family contributed to or was affected by the incest. Survivors learn that psychological problems suffered by older family members may have set the stage for incest to occur and to remain hidden. Self-blame is alleviated when survivors realize that what happened to them would have happened to any child of their sex entering the family when they did. This understanding helps free survivors from feelings of guilt and responsibility and thereby allows them to strengthen their identity apart from their family of origin.

Many survivors request clear information about family influences in order to learn how their upbringing differed from that of children in families where incest did not occur. They use this knowledge to help themselves create a different kind of life, free of destructive relationships. By reviewing their unbringing in detail, many survivors learn how to supportively "parent" themselves. This involves learning to identify and meet their physical and emotional needs themselves. As they become secure in their ability to care for themselves, survivors can then become more trusting of the caring and assistance that other people can provide. Survivors who have children can increase their ability to be good parents.

In the following sections, some common psychological stresses and relationship patterns that have been identified in incest families are presented. Much of the information comes from observation of families in which father-daughter incest occurred. Survivors who were molested by people other than their fathers will be able to identify some familiar characteristics and to adapt this information to their particular situation. (This chapter provides an overview of common traits. No family will look exactly like this and some will be quite different.)

Readers who suspect they were abused but are unable to remember any specific events may find the following information helpful in establishing whether incest did occur. While incest cannot be confirmed solely by the presence of these characteristics, it is realistic to assume that some type of inappropriate relationship may have existed if many of the characteristics are present. In some cases, the elements for abuse were present but nothing concrete ever happened, owing to lack of opportunity, the existence of minimal impulse control, or some other intervening factor. Reading this chapter may thus help some people understand why they "never felt comfortable getting a kiss from Uncle Fred," "refused to share a bed with cousin Sue," or "ran away from home at an early age."

Fathers — the Offenders

Fathers who sexually abuse their children lead double lives. On the outside they may appear no different from other fathers. They are members of every race, religion, profession, and socioeconomic group, and are of varying ages. They are often members of churches and are relatively intelligent. Many of them impress others as dedicated family men who are good providers.

Inwardly, sexually abusive fathers suffer from psychological distress, emotional isolation, and emotional immaturity. Their thinking concerning sexuality is distorted, and they lack adequate skills in impulse control. They may never have experienced a psychologically healthy life as a child. Many grew up in families where they were physically and emotionally abused by punitive, distant parents. Frequently, they themselves were victims of sexual abuse.

Sexually abusive men usually feel very inadequate and powerless. They have low self-esteem. Most do not lead self-fulfilling lives. Many feel chronically resentful toward others. They may unconsciously seek rejection and hostile responses from others as a form of self-punishment. Some seek to attain a feeling of power by exerting themselves as head of the household in a forceful and authoritarian way, resorting to violence in some cases. Other family members may feel intimidated by them. Offending fathers may become self-appointed experts on all family matters, involving themselves in the minute details of each family member's life. They are frequently successful in isolating members of the family from people outside the family. Methods for accomplishing this range from the deliberate embarrassment of guests who are visiting to directly forbidding family members to interact with others. When public disclosure of the incest occurs, outsiders may be shocked to learn that a man behaved so forcefully in private while maintaining a public persona that was very different. Other offenders acquire power by acting helpless and needy. They look as if they need to be taken care of and their victims feel sorry for them.

Sexually abusive fathers lack the ability to identify what is really bothering them, to share it with another adult, and thus to break through feelings of emotional isolation. They are weak or lacking in attributes that reflect emotional maturity, such as the ability to delay gratification, to exercise impulse control, and to empathize with another person's experience. Frequently, sexual offenders will turn to alcohol, drugs, or other forms of escape to sidestep the pain they feel inside. These behaviors further impair their functioning by lowering inhibitions and frequently go hand in hand with sexually abusive activity. Sexually abusive men turn to incest in a vain attempt to meet their emotional as well as their sexual needs.

Abusers eroticize the child by projecting sexual fantasies onto the child's body and behavior. They often masturbate while thinking of the child and thus strengthen their attraction to the child. The risky nature of the abuse, coupled with the repetition of fantasies and masturbation, serves to create heightened sexual experiences for the offender. Adrenalin that is produced by the fear of being discovered adds an intoxicating excitement. Many offenders feel powerless over their desire for this "high." They lose control of their impulses and experience their own needs as so overpowering that they ignore or deny any pain they are causing to their victims.

Distorted thinking encourages an offender to victimize the most vulnerable person available—a child who depends on him. Distorted thinking also prevents him from recognizing the harmful impact his actions are having on the child. One offender exemplified this distorted thinking by saying, "If a young child stares at my genitals, it means the child likes what he or she sees and is enjoying watching my genitals." This statement ignores the fact that young children stare at virtually everything out of the ordinary, and it implies a sexual interest of which a young child is not capable.

Sexual abusers rationalize their abusive behavior with unrealistic thoughts. These rationalizations include the idea that the offender (1) is being seduced by the child, (2) wants the child to learn about sex "properly," (3) wants the child to feel good, (4) is giving the child special attention, and (5) is not going outside the family to meet his sexual needs and is therefore keeping the family together. While none of these explanations is credible, such distorted thinking, along with the imposition of inappropriate arousal patterns on the child, allows the incest to begin. Once begun, the behavior is frequently addictive. Despite any ambivalence or desire to stop, cessation of incest is rarely attributable to the offender.

After disclosure, offenders will almost uniformly deny that the sexual abuse occurred. When the facts about the incest are presented to the offenders in such a way that they cannot deny its having occurred, they will nevertheless frequently deny responsibility for the abuse. They attempt to absolve themselves either by reiterating their unrealistic rationalizations or by blaming their spouse. However, some sexual offenders are relieved to finally be caught. The dishonesty and hidden anguish of years' duration become exposed, and they may welcome an opportunity to get control over their problems. An offender's willingness to admit his responsibility for the abuse can in itself be a big help to the victim in her recovery. It can also aid the offender in reestablishing trust with other family members, especially his spouse.

Mothers—the Nonoffending Adults

The typical mother in the incestuous family somehow conveys to her children a sense of weakened capacity. She may be overworked, chronically ill, depressed, economically dependent, and/or socially isolated. She is often a survivor of sexual abuse herself and may never have disclosed the abuse. Her ability to be responsive to her children's needs may be impaired on account of the stresses and responsibilities she feels burdened with in the family. She may be frequently absent from the house because of a demanding work schedule, or she may be busy with housework and the care of young children. Often her marriage is unsatisfying in that it may be limited in communication and emotional closeness. She may currently be in a destructive relationship with the father and may be physically abused by him. Often the mother feels intimidated by the father and may convey to her children her belief that she is not capable of asserting herself equally in that relationship.

Mothers in incestuous families may sometimes encourage their older children to assume numerous adult responsibilities that strain these children's coping abilities and reduce the amount of care and nurturance they receive. For instance, the older children may be given responsibility for care of the younger children and for household tasks. The mother may also depend heavily on her children to provide her with emotional support. The love she feels for her children may be expressed only when she is showing appreciation for what they have done for her. Mothers of incest victims may lack the ability and skills to demonstrate unconditional love. They may be unable to set aside their own neediness in order to respond with empathy to their child's daily experiences.

Disclosure of incest is a most shocking and upsetting experience for the mother. She may have had no idea that sexual abuse was going on. She may have sensed that something wasn't quite right without having allowed herself to think that it could be incest. Sometimes the mother may have doubted her own perceptions of abuse and thus may have convinced herself that she was either crazy or reading too much into an innocent situation. Often daughters do not tell their mothers about the incest because they sense the mother's weakness and want to protect her from any further pain and hardship. Daughters may also fear the loss of the family and take literally such threats as "It would kill your mother if she found out about this."

Mothers often feel immobilized at the time of disclosure. A woman may fear the disclosure means she must make a choice between her child and her husband, two people toward whom she feels love and loyalty. One woman explained her dilemma by asking, "Should I cut off my right arm or my left?"

While some mothers do respond to their daughter's disclosure in a supportive way, many frequently have a difficult time believing that incest has occurred. Some mothers totally disregard the disclosure and "forget" it was even mentioned. This amnesia-like response leaves the victim feeling ignored and invalidated. The choices a mother has to make once she accepts the incest are difficult.

> Believing that her husband or partner has abused her child or other children forces a woman to make choices and take actions. The woman who has already decided to end her relationship (either by divorce or separation) or who is on the brink of the decision is usually more likely to believe her child because she has less to lose. Sometimes learning of the abuse can precipitate a long overdue decision to end a bad relationship. The woman who wants to remain in the relationship or who at least has mixed feelings—which is most common—has the hardest time.[3]

Fully accepting that the incest occurred and learning to cope with the changes that result from it are processes that take time. Following disclosure of father-daughter incest, a mother usually goes through some or all of the following reactions:

1. She is *angry* at her daughter for not revealing the incest sooner and at her husband for doing this to her child and to her.
2. She feels *guilty* that she has failed to protect her child and that she has failed to satisfy her husband. She thinks it may be her fault that the incest has occurred.
3. She feels *betrayed* by her husband because he has been living a lie and a little by her daughter for having kept the relationship a secret.
4. She *hates* her husband for the consequences of what he has done— the damage to the child, to *her* relationship with her own child, to the relationship between herself and her husband. He is the cause of all the difficulty everyone is now experiencing.
5. She is *repulsed* by him, keeps thinking about him touching her child and trying to get the thoughts out of her mind. How could he do it?
6. Sometimes she even feels a little *jealousy* toward her daughter for the extra attention and special relationship which she seemed to have with her husband.

7. She is *confused*, because on the one hand she wants to support and help her child, but on the other hand you don't just change your feelings for someone even when you learn about sexual abuse. New feelings are competing with the old ones. She feels caught between the two sets of feelings, not sure what is best.

8. Most of all she feels that not only has she *failed* as a wife and mother but she is now *expected to take charge* of resolving all the problems that have resulted from the incest, even though she was not directly involved with the abuse or perhaps didn't even know about it at all.[4]

Mothers of incest victims find the help they need to resolve issues brought up by the disclosure when they learn to use the network of social services in their area. Parent support groups, treatment groups for mothers and victims, and educational classes on incest are effective in countering the experience of social stigma, guilt, and family disruption. With help, mothers in incestuous families can learn to be supportive of their daughters and begin to rebuild their families.

The following letter, written by a mother to her daughter, reveals the pain and growth that can come from weathering the disclosure of incest in a family.

Dearest Julie,

I am writing you this letter to help clarify my feelings and possibly open some doors of communication that have been closed to us for some time. I hope this letter can be a start for a new, open and honest relationship between us.

Julie, I want you to know that I do not blame you for any of the sexual abuse that you have gone through for the past seven years. It was Jim's fantasies that were not normal, and nothing you said or did caused Jim to sexually abuse you. Jim's fantasies started before he ever touched you. He was so subtle you weren't even aware of it when it really started.

I know the sexual touch began when you were about seven and lasted for at least seven years, starting with Jim fondling your vagina, then making you touch his penis. It got to the point were Jim would put his penis in your mouth. When you were in about the sixth grade he started getting into bed with you at night, fulfilling his fantasies by fondling you, ejaculating on you, saying sexual things to you, and attempting intercourse with you.

Some girls feel guilty because at some point they might have even enjoyed some of the sexual contact; maybe even felt like they might have wanted the attention (especially if the man is gentle). I want you to know that all of us, no matter how young, have parts of the body that are made to react to touch. And being an adult man, with sexual experience, the man knows where those spots are and how to touch them to get the reactions he wants. There is absolutely no wrongdoing on the child's part because his or her body reacts naturally, the way God intended. The problem is with the man who uses his knowledge and experience with an innocent child. Julie, I'm not even sure you have guilty feelings, but if you have any at all, please know that Jim is the adult who is completely responsible for the inappropriate sexual contact, whether it was his touching you or through any conditioning he started with you at a very early age.

Your sexuality is something very precious. I'm angry that Jim tampered with it and may have caused you to feel bad about yourself as a sexual person. If so, I hope that you can learn to feel good about yourself sexually and learn to enjoy sex under healthy circumstances in years to come.

Jim used your need for fatherly affection and attention wrongly. Instead of responding with fatherly nurturing, he sexually abused you. He would ignore you for weeks at a time, until you were starving for his attention and wondered what you had done wrong. At that point he could get you to do anything he wanted. Jim would side with you in conflicts with me. It would make me the ''bad ass'' and make you owe him; also it put us at odds, closed our communication and kept you silent. Jim always let you know he felt special towards you by buying and doing special things for you (watchband, necklaces, bookshelves, etc.). He kept John [older son] at such arm's length that the attention he showed you must have made you feel very good. All of your reaction to his manipulation was normal. It was his manipulation to abuse you that was unacceptable fatherly behavior.

I know that I must take some responsibility for what has gone on in our lives, not for the sexual abuse, but for not being there when you needed me. I know at one point, after a TV program on child abuse, you asked me what I would do if I knew Jim had touched you. My reaction was, ''I'd kill him!'' Right then I closed the door for you to tell me anything. I know my violent answer was not the help you were looking for. That answer would have scared me if the situation were reversed. I also feel that you love me very much and did not want to hurt me or break up the family. Maybe you might have felt like I might blame you by thinking you were having an affair with my husband. Julie, how could you <u>not</u> have felt thay way, I always acted so in love with Jim and always put him first. He said and did horrible things to me and I always stayed with him and just tried harder. If I did leave him, he'd talk me into coming back in a few weeks with his promises and acts of love. Julie, if Jim could manipulate me, an adult, with his actions and words, how could anyone blame you, a child, for being conned by this authority-figure adult.

I always demanded respect from you and John for him, even when you saw the emotional abuse we received from him. By doing this I reinforced his power over you and John.

I guess my biggest frustration was that not only was I not there for you, but no one was. Jim manipulated the whole family to abuse you. We all fell for his cons. He kept John at arm's length and on guard all the time. Jim was the authority over John. John could never do anything good enough to please Jim. John was always wrong—always in the way—so when Jim said jump, John jumped.

Jim used Doug and Jason [father's children from previous marriage] as an excuse to molest you. He could always tell himself that he was not going to let you or John take their place in his heart. When the boys were at our house he made sure they knew that you and John were not special and that they were still first. I guess the worse he treated you the more he felt it showed the boys they were #1.

I was always busy with Gary and Sally [youngest children, from this marriage] when they were young, so you felt neglected. Jim used your neglected feelings to molest you. He made sure I knew I never lived up to his expectations of a mother to Gary and Sally. So I was always busy trying to meet his expectations, which left you to him with more emotional needs and hurts that he could manipulate and prey on.

I know things have not worked out exactly as you've wanted since you disclosed to me about Jim's sexual abuse to you. All I can say is, I am so grateful you were brave enough to tell me so it could be stopped. I want you to know that everything that has happened to our family after disclosure is completely Jim's doing. He was the one who put our family on the line. It's because of his actions that the family is separated. It's because of his actions that he was sent to jail. It was because of his actions we may not be together as a family for Christmas. The result of his actions are what caused all the confusion in our lives. I know this and I want you to know it too.

I could write a book on the ways Jim has used our family. There are so many instances I recall, now that I know Jim was manipulating all of us to sexually abuse you. I did not recognize the characteristics or the manipulation for what it was until I received group counseling. I knew there was something wrong but just couldn't put my finger on what it was. Through the teaching and counseling with the mothers' group, I'm finally understanding. Neither you nor I was to blame for Jim's actions. He was; and it's up to him to change them. But we can change our relationship with each other to an open and honest one so neither Jim nor anyone else can ever hurt us in this way again. Let's talk about all the instances that Jim manipulated and used power over us. Let's open ourselves up to each other so you will know you can trust me to protect you always. Let's learn how to stop this in this generation so none of our babies to come will go through what you have.

I love you so,

Mama

Children — the Victims

Child victims in incestuous families live in an ongoing state of psychological stress. They are generally unhappy children. They are troubled by memories of past abuse, fears of future abuse, and the pressure to keep the sexual experiences secret. The psychological stress of the abuse is seen most often by a change in the child's behavior, which may occur at the onset of the sexual abuse or which may develop as the child grows older.

The following behaviors may be present in children who are victims of sexual abuse.

Common signs in young children include: nightmares and other sleeping disturbances; bedwetting, fecal soiling; excessive masturbation; clinging/whining; regression to more infantile behavior; explicit sexual knowledge, behavior, or language unusual for their age; withdrawal; frequent genital infections; unexplained gagging; agitation/hyperactivity/irritability/aggressiveness; loss of appetite.

Common signs in older children include: depression; withdrawal; poor self-image; chemical abuse; running away or aversion to going home; recurrent physical complaints, such as infections, cramping or abdominal pains, muscle aches, dizziness, gagging and severe headaches; self-mutilations such as cutting, burning, tattooing, suicide attempts; truancy; change in school performance; overtly seductive behavior/promiscuity/prostitution; eating disorders such as anorexia, sudden weight gain or loss; limited social life; attention-getting or delinquent behavior.[5]

It is not uncommon for these signs to be completely ignored by other family members. If there is a response, it often consists of blaming or punishing the child for the behavior. One woman shared that she pulled all her eyelashes out beginning at the time her father started molesting her. Her mother called it a bad habit and scolded her to stop; she lacked the education and sensitivity to know that these behaviors can be symptoms of sexual abuse. Thus it is not surprising that the actual abuse may go undetected for a long time.

Victims of abuse grow up without a sense of protection and security. All children need the security of feeling protected from danger in the world in order to build inner strength and to venture into new experiences. Victims of abuse do not trust that the adults in their lives can place a child's welfare before their own. As victims mature, they may be handicapped in their ability to establish trusting relationships with others. Sexual abuse conveys the message to the child that the offender's needs come first, so it destroys the basis for child-adult trust. The abuser teaches the child that it is not safe to trust. It is a harsh lesson to discover that the same person who is supposed to protect you in life is the person who is harming you the most. Trust may be further impaired by a lack of responsiveness on the part of the nonoffending parent, who does not protect the child from the abuse.

Like all children, victims of sexual abuse are vulnerable and dependent on others. They accept the attitudes and beliefs of the older people in the family as truth. Quite understandably, they are not able to perceive a larger view of their experience, one which would indicate that something in the family as a whole is very wrong.

The abused child may assume that the abuse is something she caused or deserved. All young children view themselves as the center of all their experiences. It is difficult for the child to realize that the abuse has very little to do with her, that it is a symptom of a sickness no one can see in the offender.

Lacking perspective, the child may believe that all families are like hers and that children are commonly sexually abused by older family members. One woman remarked, "I thought it [the sex] was just another part of growing up. I imagined my friends had to do it too." In contrast, many victims may feel strongly that something is wrong but, because of their immaturity, are unable to verbalize the experience or act to stop the abuse.

Methods used by the offender to coerce the child into sexual behavior and keep that behavior secret impact negatively on the child's sense of well-being. The inherent imbalance of power in the adult-child relationship establishes a basis for coercion. It doesn't take much more than action on the part of the offender to obtain the child's cooperation. Some children are forced into incest through various forms of physical abuse, such as being slapped, hit, drugged, and held down. When physical force is used, fear and pain may increase to extreme levels. Sexual energy may become infused with associations to violent energy. Once this association is learned, the victim has a hard time separating the two types of energy.

Many child victims are coerced into secretive sexual activity by nonphysical pressure tactics. These may include subtle nonverbal approaches such as silent, occasional fondling during bedtime play and touching the child's breasts or genitals when the child is thought to be asleep. One woman described how all her father had to do was look at her with his "sad puppy-dog eyes." Another woman said her grandfather would silently, expressionlessly walk over to her when they were alone. Nothing was said; these women knew what "the look" meant and knew they had no choice. Nonphysical methods of pressure also include a wide variety of verbal means, including commanding, threatening, bribing, and pleading with the child. Some offenders explain to the children that the activity is a form of sex education, that it's a punishment, or that it is acceptable, common behavior.

Some offenders are well aware of the emotional neediness of the child. They may use their awareness for the purpose of manipulating the child into sex. They may give and withhold privileges, love, and acceptance in order to obtain the child's cooperation.

Child victims in incestuous families often long for adult love and attention. Quite frequently, adult survivors report that they were neglected by all the adults in their lives except the offender. When this type of relationship occurs (where the offender was the primary, only nurturing, caring adult in their lives) an intense protective loyalty may be apparent. Even after the abuse becomes public, the child may defend and continue to idealize the offender. Their emotional dependency on the offender may blind them to the harm caused by the abuse.

Child victims in incestuous families are likely to have assumed a role as a parentlike figure to other family members. This process, known in psychological terms as parentification, involves the child feeling responsibility for the family's welfare. A survivor described the role reversal in her family in this way: "I aligned with my mother, but my mother never really aligned with me. I was there to protect her, and she was very childlike and I was very parental toward her." Since the victim is frequently the oldest daughter in the family, those girls who have become the "little mother" of the house may submit to sexual abuse in order to keep the offender from abusing a younger sibling or physically hurting their mother. Other victims, keenly aware of the family's financial dependency on the offender, may assume that the sexual contact is necessary to obtain basic survival needs such as food, shelter, and clothing.

Offenders understand the implications of parental behavior in children and may emphasize how the child will be responsible if the offender goes to jail, if the family breaks up, if the mother has a nervous breakdown, or if the younger child gets taken away. The offender may also appeal to the victim's sense of responsibility and power by asking how she can deny her lonely father his only source of pleasure. These comments serve as powerful silencers and discourage disclosure.

Feelings of low self-esteem, fear, hopelessness, depression, and responsibility hold the child victim back from disclosing the incest. Sometimes the child suppresses the incest from her conscious memory. Often the child just hopes the sexual abuse will stop on its own or tries to avoid situations in which it may come up. Victims may fear that no change will occur after disclosure and that their family's lack of caring for them will be confirmed. Others fear that too much change will occur. One woman, abused from age three to seventeen by her father, stepfather, brother, and uncle, explained:

> I thought I'd be blamed and shamed—I had a crush on my stepfather, so I thought I caused it at age five. When I was older, a teen, I thought my mother would have a nervous breakdown or else kill someone, or some unknown and horribly shameful catastrophe would happen. We were not emotionally close. I lived in a fantasy world for survival. . . . I was under *extreme* stress. I felt suicidal, homicidal, and schizophrenic. Barely on the edge of sanity, *constantly.*

When a child victim is able to disclose immediately following the first incident, it's a sign that she feels positive about herself and that she generally feels supported in the family.

Too frequently the child's worst fears are borne out and disclosure is met with shrugged shoulders, blame, punishment, and continued incest. When family members react in these ways, it leads to deeper feelings of depression and hopelessness for the victim. One survivor related that her disclosure precipitated her parents' divorce but the incest did not stop. The actual experience of disclosure can be very upsetting to a child, owing to confrontations with police, social workers, and juvenile authorities. Personal emotional support from at least one relative is extremely important for minimizing feelings of guilt and confusion.

Disclosure can be a very helpful experience if it stops further abuse, frees the child from the necessity of having to maintain a self-defeating secret, and provides public recognition and validation of the injustice done to the child. Whether or not disclosure occurs, the child is often left with mixed feelings toward the offender. She may feel both love and disgust for him at the same time. As adults some women continue some of the incest dynamics by feeling a need to please their fathers. Feelings of intense rage may be covered up when the adult survivor continues to play the role of the responsible, loving daughter.

Family Patterns

Families in which incest occurs tend to be closed, inward families lacking in real emotional connection to people outside the family. The couple is usually not working together well as spouses or parents. They may have an active sex life but usually lack emotional intimacy.

These families often have a history of problems for several generations which increase the potential for incest. Frequently, the mothers of abuse victims were themselves sexually molested as children. The majority of offenders have a history of sexual abuse, physical abuse, or emotional abandonment in their families of origin. Alcoholism, a documented hereditary disease, often seems to travel from one generation to the next, along with incestuous behavior. Family patterns that allow alcoholism to continue untreated for many years similarly foster undetected sexual abuse.

Family members learn roles of victim and perpetrator which become accepted and commonplace. Children pick up on the intimidation, fear, and helplessness the nonoffending adult feels toward the perpetrator. This limits the options children perceive for getting out of the abusive relationship. Many victims assume that being dominated and treated poorly by the offender is just a fact of life, not something to be challenged. Perpetrators of abuse desperately attempt to avoid their own feelings of helplessness by doing what as children they associated with being powerful—dominating and manipulating others in the family. But because they still view themselves as victims, they fail to assume responsibility for their own abusive behaviors. It is impossible for them to consider relinquishing their position of dominance, as this is their only fragile hold on power. Giving it up would force them to face the flood of fear, anger, and vulnerability which they have repressed from childhood.

How is incest passed down in families? While the following scenario is just one of many possibilities, it does provide insight into the influence that family patterns can have on incest.

A typical pattern might include a father who is needy and dependent and has unusually high expectations of being taken care of by his family. The mother is also needy and exhausted. There is little emotional intimacy between the parents. The father was abused by his own family as a child and finds close contact with his oldest daughter sexually arousing. She has taken on more and more responsibility for household tasks and child care to relieve her mother, who is overwhelmed. The daughter has often been told by her parents to do as she is told and not question her parents. The father tells her she is special and may give her more attention than the other children. She feels close to him and appreciates his affection. The affectionate touch gradually changes from tickling to massage to sexual fondling to oral sex. The father tells her it is her duty to take care of him. The mother consciously ignores signs of abuse, unable to face its consequences. The daughter grows up feeling dirty and different from other girls. She does not "tell" because it has been going on for so long that she is afraid of being blamed and does not think anyone will believe her. Her self-esteem is poor, and escape from home becomes a goal. She chooses a partner who looks strong, expecting that he will take care of her. His neediness attracts her; she is familiar with needy men and wants to be loved. Her partner's "strength" is often a coverup for his own insecurity. They marry, slowly become alienated and depressed, and have children who once again fall prey to incest.

There are many variations in family incest patterns and, like the example just given, they often involve families being socially isolated, being run in an authoritarian manner, and adhering to limiting male and female roles. Severe family stress can make families more susceptible to abuse. Stress hampers people's ability to make good decisions and to exert impulse control over inappropriate tendencies. Family influences may contribute to incest, but the offender's behavior *is* the abuse. The offender is the sole person responsible for the abuse.

As adults, survivors have two major tasks to accomplish in relation to family influences: the resolution of intense feelings and the establishment of new boundaries with old family members. Resolving the intense, leftover feelings from the abuse allows survivors to close the incest chapter in their lives and move on to create better relationships and better times. Feelings such as anger, fear, betrayal, and sadness need to come to the surface and be expressed in safe, supportive ways. Sometimes this can occur directly, when family members are willing to be involved. Many times it is more appropriate for it to occur indirectly through therapy, either because of the lack of availability and supportiveness of other family members or in order to avoid negative consequences for the survivor. This letting go of old feelings frees the survivor from the victim role she may have played in the family. Understanding and resolving feelings allows her to live a life unencumbered by continual bitterness and hatred.

How a survivor chooses to establish adult relationships with the offender and other family members is an individual decision based on a variety of circumstances. The key is that the survivor needs to give herself permission to limit contact, and possibly to change the whole nature of the contact if that's what she requires to affirm her separateness and strength. Distancing emotionally, physically, and even geographically may be very appropriate. Many survivors only feel comfortable reestablishing contact after they have gained assertiveness and self-protection skills, have learned to reduce their expectations of how much closeness is possible, and have lessened their need for love and support from their family of origin.

Survivors often wonder whether they should feel forgiveness toward the offender and other members of the family. Forgiveness in the sense of releasing others from responsibility for their harmful actions and believing that the actions were justified is not healthy. But if forgiveness can be defined in a way that emphasizes understanding a person's humanness, limitations, and history, then it may be very beneficial. This second style of forgiveness is self-affirming. It can allow and encourage the survivor to accept her own humanness, develop compassion toward herself, remove remaining self-blame, and release herself from constantly experiencing negative feelings toward old family members. The issue of forgiveness is something each survivor must resolve for herself.

4
How Survivors Coped during Molestation

During molestation incest victims are subject to high degrees of stress—mentally and physically. They may be flooded with feelings of fear, panic, confusion, and betrayal, and may suffer from enormous anxiety. Victims may strain to find reasons why the incest is happening, as well as ways to stop it. Since children's bodies are undeveloped and unprepared for sexual activity, the physical sensations of the abuse can be overwhelming, creating discomfort, unbearable pain, or unusual pleasures. Each victim learns to cope with the stress of incest in her own fashion. This chapter will discuss some coping methods survivors have used during molestation. It will also describe the role these methods later played in hampering sexual satisfaction. Problems can arise when survivors continue to employ old coping methods in adult sexual relations where there is no longer any threat to their well-being. Since coping methods were developed during traumatic situations, they tend to be deeply ingrained and hard to let go of.

Coping methods are critical ways victims find to protect their sense of well-being and personal integrity. Because of the intense stress of sexual abuse, failure to employ coping methods could seriously jeopardize a victim's sanity and will to live. Human beings need to feel some amount of control over their experiences in order to maintain individual identity. An incest experience traps the victim and then forces her to submit to the will of the offender. Panic and desperation result in a triggering of her primal instincts for survival, which include a desire to fight the offender or flee from the abuse. However, given the dynamics of incest and the size and power differences between the victim and the offender, these options are rarely available.

People who were never sexually abused can learn to empathize with what survivors experienced by recalling episodes of tickling in childhood. The following exercise for nonsurvivors is designed for that purpose: Remember those times when you were held down and tickled, and the tickling became too much, too intense. Laughing may have quickly turned to panic as you cried out, "Stop it, it hurts!" The experience of feeling out of control and overstimulated easily turned something fun and pleasurable into something very uncomfortable and frightening. Imagine further how much worse the situation would have been if you had felt unable to say "Stop!" or if your pleas had gone unattended.

Lacking other alternatives, incest victims must rely on indirect methods of self-protection. These methods help them to survive the ordeal of the abuse while it is occurring. While coping methods may vary, they all appear to facilitate mental escape from the abuse or relief from the stress of physical sensations.

A common coping method used by victims during incest is a process known as dissociation. Victims dissociate from the incest by divorcing themselves mentally from the experience. Dissociation permits them to blank out and be somewhere else in their minds. They create a mind-body split so they do not have to stay mentally present and fully experience the discomfort or pain of the abuse. They may quickly lose the memory or have only vague, dreamlike recall of what happened to them. So victims may end up feeling that whatever happened didn't really happen to them. Because dissociation can block an important experience from conscious memory, survivors are sometimes left not feeling fully themselves in many other situations. The desire to separate themselves from the experience of incest may result in impaired memory function in general. Survivors who used dissociation to cope with their pain may be especially prone to the problem of not remembering the incest at all as adults. Dissociation helps survivors fulfill a deep wish to believe the incest never really happened.

The importance of dissociation in maintaining a sense of personal control and power is graphically demonstrated by the following case. A client showed her therapist a photograph of herself being vaginally raped by her father and anally raped by her brother at the same time. The picture was taken by her sister under the direction of her father. In the picture the victim was lying back, expressionlessly filing her nails. She focused her attention and control on a part of her body that was not being invaded.

When dissociation becomes an automatic response to sexual stimulation, it can have the serious consequence of inhibiting sexual pleasure. This is illustrated by a client whose father had intercourse with her once a week after school. During these episodes she would concentrate all her awareness on the sounds of children playing outside the house. She vividly imagined herself being with them instead of with her father. As a consequence, in adult life she had difficulty remembering sexual experiences with her husband. She had learned amnesia as a response to sexual contact. In therapy she concentrated on recalling and safely reliving the sexual details of the incest. Once she was able to accomplish this, she found herself able to recall and accept enjoyment from sexual experiences with her husband.

Another survivor mentioned using techniques of intense concentration to dissociate at will from the incest trauma. Although her current sexual relationship was very supportive, she still found herself leaving her body to avoid feelings associated with the past sexual abuse.

> There are times when we have sex together that I find myself checking out of the sex. There's a plant that hangs above our bed, and that's what I will usually do—find a spot up on the ceiling or on the wall or the corner of the room or something. I will just kind of try to go there. Once in a while we'll get going, and I feel like something's going to come up and I can feel that I do it again. But it's not anything that's really creating a problem with us, because I think I'm to a point where I'm coming alive sexually.

Extreme forms of dissociation are evident in some survivors who establish a mind-body split that causes them to leave the physical reality of a sexual situation and enter into a state totally unrelated to who and where they are at the time. One survivor explained:

> During incest, penetration was always painful, but I could ignore it and laugh it off. . . . [Now] I never withdraw my body from the scene—my mind always distorts the real scene in order to protect myself. My body doesn't have to fear because my mind leaves and my body becomes an object. When my mind is in total control, my body then joins my mind somewhere else. Then this is happening outside *my* body—orgasm happens, but it is not my body. It is someone else, somewhere else, in another place and time.

Survivors who divorce themselves to this extent sometimes experience difficulty with their ability to control this extreme dissociative response. They may become vulnerable to developing multiple personality problems. One study of people with multiple personality disorders found that 83 percent of the subjects had experienced sexual abuse as children; of these, 68 percent had been victims of incest.[6]

Other forms of dissociation used as coping methods are aimed at withstanding intense physical pain and violence. Some victims report having been able consciously to induce a numbing of parts of their bodies. Others created pain in their bodies that they could focus on during the abuse in order to distract themselves from the pain being caused by the perpetrators — for example, by biting their lip or holding their breath. In some cases survivors have been able to transform the pain they felt into some other sensation, as one woman explained:

> The pain turned to comfort after a while because I conditioned my mind to accept pain as pleasure and warmth so it didn't hurt anymore. He needed to see how much fear and pain I could endure without crying, and it made him so angry that I wouldn't cry. He couldn't hurt me in any way physically. But emotionally he did.

The process of dissociating can become so ingrained that it can be generalized for use in other times of stress, such as taking physical exams and sustaining injuries. There are cases of incest survivors who have been able to induce self-hypnotic anesthesia. One girl taught herself to do this at age eleven while her stepfather was squeezing four fingers of her hand until she cried. The girl, as described by Denise Gelinas,

> remembered looking straight into his eyes and holding her breath so that this time she wouldn't cry, telling herself not to feel her hand. As she began feeling the pressure of her lack of breath, it became easier not to feel her hand. Later that night, the stepfather came into the bathroom and asked to see that hand. She put it down on the edge of the sink and he abruptly brought his fist down onto it. The patient states that during the short interval of time between the beginning of his motion and the impact, she had been able to "not feel" her hand. Since that episode she has been able to induce and reinforce anesthesia when she felt she needed it.[7]

While numbing the body can be an important protection during times of physical pain, it can also create a serious disruption in a survivor's ability to become sexually aroused and to experience sexual pleasure. Survivors who have acquired these critical skills in order to deal with pain in their childhood are faced as adults with the challenge of slowly sensitizing their bodies and letting in the good sensations that they have a right to experience.

Repeated bouts of physical pain and unwanted touching may leave a person fearful of all kinds of touching. Positive associations with touching, such as feeling soothed, comforted, or reassured, get replaced by a pervasive feeling of mistrust, leaving the survivor wondering what will follow after the gentle touching. Incest survivors may find themselves unable to feel comfortable with a simple hug. Their bodies may become automatically rigid or limp when they are approached. They learn to assume that touching is for someone else's benefit instead of their own.

Many survivors turn to alcohol and drugs to help themselves escape mentally and physically during the incest. Conscious awareness is numbed as survivors seek to transport themselves far from the horrible feeling of being out of control. One survivor described drinking alcohol and taking drugs almost every night from age twelve onward. During the period of the incest, she would do this until she obtained a state of semiconsciousness so that when her father entered her room she could be less aware of what he was doing to her. Subsequent sexual experiences with other partners were undertaken only if she was drugged. She had become so used to sex this way that once she made a commitment to sobriety, the thought of sober sexual interaction was terrifying. This survivor had to learn how to be present, in control, and responsive almost from scratch.

Some survivors pretend to be sleeping during the abuse. They shut their eyes and make their bodies go completely limp. This response allows them to express their power indirectly, by preventing the perpetrator from gaining the satisfaction of experiencing their wakeful submission. These survivors become adept at sublimating their feelings and reactions during sex.

Responding to sexual stimulation is another important coping method used during sexual abuse. Feeling pleasure allows a victim to get relief from the tension of stimulation and thus enables her to take care of herself. Unfortunately, the repercussions of this enjoyment can be very upsetting later on. These victims may have a hard time believing that the sexual contact constituted abuse, since they enjoyed it and may even have sought it once it began. They may begin to doubt their role in the abuse and wonder whether they in fact wanted it to occur. Sexual contact does not have to be violent, painful, or always unwanted to constitute abuse. It is abuse if victims are robbed of their sexual innocence and manipulated into premature sex for someone else's benefit.

When early sexual experiences are perceived as both pleasurable and repugnant, there may be a sense of betrayal by one's own body. Self-hatred toward one's body and genitals can result. Some survivors have expressed dismay at the fact that during incest they became highly aroused and achieved orgasm. All this means is that their genitals were responding appropriately to sexual stimulation. The sensitive nerve endings are not capable of determining who is touching or the circumstances under which the touching occurs. Sexual arousal can occur in many inappropriate situations. It is natural for human bodies to respond to sexual touching. Given effective stimulation, it is difficult to inhibit arousal and orgasm. Being psychologically repulsed by what is happening is often not enough to counter a physiological response. Survivors who responded physiologically with pleasure may later avoid sex or minimize arousal to prevent having to reexperience the memory of the incest. It is important for these survivors to realize that their bodies were not at fault. The sensations were positive; it was the coercion and aspect of betrayal in the experience that were negative. Adults can make choices about when to act on sexual arousal. Children forced into sexual activity don't have that choice and can consequently become very confused by their response.

Many of the medical and sexual problems that survivors experience later in life have their roots in the sexual trauma. It is common for survivors to complain of recurring physical ailments such as migraines, vaginal pain, back pain, neck pain, and skin problems. Survivors who were forced to have oral sex sometimes suffer from jaw, neck, and throat problems. Those who were penetrated often report such complaints as recurrent vaginal infections, severe menstrual pain, and painful intercourse. Occasionally survivors will feel that they were permanently impaired by the physical attacks. For instance, a survivor who had never experienced orgasm believed the incest had broken her clitoris and made it dysfunctional.

Protection skills are a very important and creative means with which survivors deal with abuse. They are very positive and absolutely necessary. They become problems only when the situation has changed and they are no longer useful, that is, when they continue to be used after the incest has stopped. Spacing out during sex is an important protection for a child but becomes an unwelcome obstruction for an adult woman. It is important for survivors to remember that these methods of coping were learned. New ways of feeling safe can now be learned.

A first step in this process is identifying and understanding the old coping methods. Adult survivors *can* regain the ability to be present and can integrate their mind and body in a way that will allow them to feel comfort, pleasure, control, and a sense of security with sexual touching.

5
Effects of Incest on Self-Concept

During childhood, incest experiences hinder the development of high self-esteem and good self-image. The immediate effects of the trauma of incest are often fear and immobilization. The impact is even more significant because the incest often lasts a long time and may not be addressed for years. It can lead to chronic depression, guilt, a sense of powerlessness, and poor self-esteem. These feelings may be manifested in many self-destructive activities, such as alcohol and drug abuse, suicide attempts, and sexual relationships in which the woman continues to be victimized.

Understanding how the incest has such a strong impact on the development of self-concept can help survivors begin to feel better about themselves and reclaim their sexuality. A child's self-concept is built by taking in messages from the important adults in her life. When she is praised, supported, and encouraged, she will come to believe she is worth praising, supporting, and encouraging. She will probably like herself and feel she is worthwhile. In contrast, a child who gets the message that what she feels and wants doesn't count will come to feel that she is not lovable. She may feel discouraged and believe she does not deserve to be cared for by others. Her basic sense of self-worth can easily become associated with her ability to second-guess the needs of other people in her family. Being sensitive to others' needs brings her praise from the family and helps her avoid family upset, which is distressing to her. In the process of becoming adept at sensing how others are thinking and feeling, she may learn to discount and invalidate her own needs. The unsupported child may strive to be perfect in the eyes of her family. She may incorrectly come to believe that any misery she experiences is her own fault. As one survivor recounted:

I believed in perfection and strove to obtain it. But it was a hard life—trying so hard and always coming up short of the mark. I was disappointed in myself because I kept letting myself get in the way of perfection. I was limiting myself. I was frustrated by not knowing how to overcome my weaknesses and by making the same mistakes time after time. I felt guilty for each imperfection I had, and that guilt weighed heavily on my shoulders, dragging me down to where my eyes were directed to the ground instead of being able to look up, out, and around. I wasn't able to see that overall, I was really okay, and so was my world.

An unsupported child is not a different kind of person from a child who receives support. They have just received different messages on a daily basis for many years. They have both learned to believe what they heard.

An incest survivor learns not to expect reciprocity in relationships. Because she is expected to meet the needs of the family and the perpetrator at the expense of her own, she learns that others don't really care to respond to her inner concerns. Her sense of importance is perceived as equivalent to her actions as a giver. She gives to everyone but herself. Her physical needs for caring touching and for affection may remain unmet. She may not give herself permission to ask for the kind of nurturance she really wants. Her participation in physical touching may be limited to times when she feels sexually exploited.

Incest is particularly damaging to self-concept in another way as well: victims are systematically forced to doubt their own perceptions of reality. Adults guide children by validating children's perceptions. For example, a parent may agree with a child that the water is hot or the dog is dangerous, as the child suspected. Children gain self-esteem by trusting their own feelings and experiences and by being believed by others. This makes it possible for them to act on their beliefs. In incest, the offender is so involved in his own experience that the victim's perceptions get discredited and denied. Sandy Solomon, an incest therapist, explains: "There is lying and deception by the parent . . . and if the child believes the parent's lie to be the truth, then she will have to believe her experiential truth to be a lie."

It is very painful and difficult for a child to perceive her parent as a liar. To seriously doubt a parent's honesty shakes up the trust system the child has for understanding the world. Even though the thinking of the offender is distorted by his addiction, the child generally doesn't realize this at the time. It's not uncommon for an abuser to tell the victim that she is to blame for the incest. When a victim protests that she doesn't like what's going on, the abuser may respond by insisting that she does like it. One teen's father, after she told him she did not like what he was doing to her, replied, "Yes, you do. You know you do, you little tease!" Interactions like these leave the child with a sense of self-doubt and with a limited ability to trust herself. The offender benefits from the child's confusion, because children who doubt themselves are more vulnerable and more easily tricked into further sexual interaction and secrecy.

The following excerpt from a teen survivors' group illustrates the influence of the offender's thinking on the child's developing self-concept.

LEADER: What things did your fathers or stepfathers tell you about sex or tell you about your body?

GIRL 1: Well, what he told me was that I would never have a boyfriend if I didn't make out with him. He said guys wouldn't like me and, for example, if a guy took me out to dinner I would have to pay him back somehow. That's just like being a hooker or something; you've got to give a little and take a little. That's exactly what it is. I'd like to go into modeling as soon as I get my teeth straightened, but my dad would always show me pictures of naked girls in *Playboy* magazines. He'd ask me if I knew who the girls were, and I'd tell him I didn't, and he'd tell me that she was so-and-so's girlfriend, and another was so-and-so's wife. My dad said that he would be my manager if when I got older I would try to get into *Playboy*. He said I'd be a big model and make movies and everything. When I was younger, I didn't know what a prostitute was, and my dad would tell me that they were girls who would stand on street corners and sell their bodies and there were guys who managed them and they would get to live in fancy apartments and wear fancy clothes and buy fancy cars. He said all I would have to do was what I was doing to him, and he was showing me how to do it so I would be able to get ahead in life.

LEADER: Most fathers don't want their daughters to be prostitutes.

GIRL 1: He would probably have been my pimp if I'd let him. He just lies so much that it really makes me mad.

GIRL 2: My dad used to ask me if it felt good. I'd tell him that it felt terrible, but he'd say that it felt good to him and he'd tell me that when I got older and started developing that it would feel really good and that I'd want him to do it to me. And I was saying that I didn't like it and didn't want him to do it to me.

LEADER: And so, again, the message was that you were there to meet his sexual needs; it didn't matter that you didn't like it or that it hurt you—it was pleasing to him, and that was all that mattered.

GIRL 2: Yeah. I would ask him why he was doing it to me, and he would tell me he did it because it made him feel good. I told him that it didn't make me feel good and that it wasn't really fair, and he'd remind me of all the presents he gave me. If we were shopping and I'd see a dress or a pair of shoes that I liked, he'd ask me if I wanted them. When I'd say yes, he'd tell me that if I did this and this and this with him he'd get me the things. Or he'd tell me if I did something with him, he'd give me such-and-such an amount of money, and if I did another thing, he'd give me another amount of money, and if he could take pictures of me I'd get money also.

GIRL 1: And that really makes you feel like a hooker because you're giving something and you're getting paid for it just like they do. Maybe not quite as much, but it really makes your self-image a lot lower.

This is an example of how the offender tries to bend the perceptions of the victim. The father of Girl 1 twisted her desire to become a model into a willingness to become a prostitute under his management and made incest seem necessary for learning basic skills to attain her goals. In the case of Girl 2, the offender discounted her experience of the sexual abuse and tried to plant ideas of how she would feel about it in the future in an effort to justify his actions. She had been consistently taught by the offender to take bribes for activities that she didn't want to engage in, and thus she learned to devalue her own perceptions and weaken her personal sense of integrity.

Another way in which an offender may have influenced the child's developing image of herself is through the use of such labels as "sexy whore," "bitch," "baby doll," or "evil one." These can leave bitter scars on the victim's self-concept. They sink into the child's mind below the conscious level and change the child's feeling about herself. Survivors need to realize that these terms served to sexually arouse the offender or to allow the offender to convince himself that he was not responsible for what he was doing. The terms are *not* reflective of who the victim really was or who the survivor really is now.

Even when the offender made complimentary comments about the victim during the abuse, the comments created confusion concerning the victim's perception of herself. Positive comments were usually viewed with suspicion and disbelief. Here are a few examples from the teen survivors' group:

> He always told me I was really beautiful, but I never could quite believe him, because whenever you look in the mirror at yourself you always see this ugly image of yourself. I thought he was just saying that to make me feel better about myself so that I would do what he wanted me to.
>
> What I got was a comparison between my mom and me. He'd say my breasts were so much fuller and firmer than my mom's, or my body was so much more supple, and all this, which didn't really say anything about me as a person; it was just in comparison to my mom. I really don't know what he could expect, because during most of it, my mom was pregnant.

In some cases, victims enjoyed hearing complimentary comments. They may have liked hearing that they were more attractive and nicer than other women. Given their loneliness, they may have enjoyed receiving special attention, praise, and displays of affection. For these women, feelings of guilt and anger can surface later and erase any positive influence the earlier compliments may have had on self-concept formation. The source of the compliments was not trustworthy.

Many survivors report having strong negative feelings toward their bodies; "ugly," "repulsive," and "disgusting" are words victims frequently use to describe themselves. These feelings serve to fuel their self-hatred and guilt. Survivors may respond to having negative feelings about their bodies in a variety of ways. They may hide their bodies with excessive weight, clothes, and hairstyles; may neglect their grooming and/or hygiene; may flaunt their bodies with seductive dress; may harm their bodies by taking extreme physical risks or by abusing drugs and alcohol; or may fail to nourish and generally care for themselves in a healthy way. These actions serve to illustrate to themselves and to others the diminished value they see in themselves.

Objectifying their bodies can become so routine to some survivors that they will jeopardize their health or discount their natural beauty in ways that would cause most women to cringe. One client bleached her hair blonde and had breast implants inserted because her husband liked women who looked that way. She was in her fifth pregnancy, although she had been advised by her doctor that having another baby could kill her. She wanted this child so her husband could finally have a girl.

Years of self-doubt and poor self-image take their toll on survivors by fostering emotional and social isolation. Many survivors did poorly in school, as they were unable to concentrate and were often depressed and discouraged. In speaking about how the incest and subsequent courtroom ordeal affected her sense of self-esteem, one survivor said:

> I hated myself and couldn't get along with others. I was always getting into trouble at school for fighting. My life was miserable. I got poor grades and spent most of my time alone. I retreated from life. When I was at home I spent most of my time in my bedroom, usually crying. I wanted to belong. I wanted to have friends, but I had established a reputation for being a poor sport and a fighter. I was a loner. During recess I sat by myself. I knew the other kids didn't want to play with me. I was a social reject, a complete outcast.
>
> In the sixth grade I was a total reject. I was always late for school. I rarely had homework done on time. I was irresponsible. I was always forgetting everything. I wore hand-me-down clothes that were outdated. My hair was unkempt and I didn't care for myself. I had tried to change over the years, but something always held me back.

Some survivors become super-achievers who put their energy into trying to gain a positive sense of themselves through work accomplishments. But old beliefs often make satisfaction with their achievements difficult. A survivor remarked:

> Even though I have had academic success, there are times when I feel like my I.Q. is below average. I wonder if really I'm a dumb person trying to be smart. However, at other times, I remind myself that I have gotten good grades in school, so I must have some brains.

Learned self-doubt may extend into a survivor's adult life, making her prey to abusive partners and to the feeling that she is unable to trust her own perceptions. All along the way, each failure or perceived failure provides further evidence for her belief that she is different from and not as good as other people.

For survivors riddled with unresolved concerns about trust, early relationships in childhood and adolescent years can be rocky or non-existent. The mother of a survivor explained that her daughter seemed to have intense, close relationships that lasted for only a few months. Her daughter would lie to her friends and try to manipulate them, and sooner or later the friends would decide they had had enough. Group therapy helped the daughter to change this pattern.

As teens, some survivors established very healthy relationships with teachers, relatives, or friends that helped them through the rough times and gave them a sense of self-worth and lovableness. The importance of these relationships cannot be overemphasized. Here a survivor describes her first major friendship:

> At the end of my sixth-grade year I met a girl named Jane Smith. I was sitting by myself at recess, as usual, when she came and sat down beside me. She started talking with me, and I found it easy to talk to her. Before I knew it, she had invited me over to her house. From that day forth, we were best of friends, and still are to this day. We spent all of that summer together. I was then eleven years old. Jane believed in me, and I loved her. We needed each other. We spent many days at her house singing while she played the guitar. That fall, Jane and I started junior high school together. We were excited about going to a new school. For me it was a new beginning. I made lots of friends and found that people liked me. Without trying, I averaged B grades in my classes. One of the high points in my life was when I received an A grade in my seventh-grade health class. I felt really good about myself. For the first time I felt like I could succeed. This is when I decided I wanted to be an A student, and I have been ever since. I know now that if I try hard enough at something, I can obtain my goal. I feel good when I learn new things, and I like school. My twelfth year was when I was the happiest. I had friends, and I liked myself.

How girls feel about being female and going through puberty may also be affected by the incest. Some girls reported blaming their bodies for "causing" the incest. One teen incest survivor said, "I wished I was a man; then I wouldn't have cramps anymore, my boobs wouldn't be in the way, and he wouldn't have touched me." Indeed, reaching puberty can be a fearful experience for a victim. Menstruation may have brought with it the fear or reality of pregnancy. Developing secondary sexual characteristics may have signaled the onset or acceleration of the abuse. This rejection of female identity because of the incest disrupts the process of self-acceptance so important to the development of positive self-esteem.

The development of an eating disorder that results in extreme thinness or in an overweight condition may be an unconscious reaction to the incest and a way of avoiding the acceptance of sexual maturity in young adulthood. Extreme thinness can cause menstruation to cease and can give the female a boyish appearance, with undeveloped breasts and practically no hips. Overeating can also produce a body that is less attractive and thus less vulnerable to the sexual interests of others. While serving as a protective function for survivors, these extreme conditions seriously jeopardize health and reinforce feelings of social isolation, rejection, and inadequacy. A large number of people suffering from eating disorders were victims of incest.

Some survivors have an internal image of their body that became fixed at the age when the incest occurred. Looking in a mirror at themselves in the present, they may be surprised to find fully developed bodies along with obvious signs of aging, such as wrinkles. One survivor explained:

> I experience something I call the Alice in Wonderland phenomenon, where I experience my body in different sizes. . . thinking for one moment I am too young to drive, too young to go out on a date, etc., or coming out with a five-year-old's voice when I speak.

In our study, women had many ideas about how they might be different if they had not been incest victims. They felt that they would have:

been more trusting

known their personal power better

had better self-images

been more successful

been more relaxed

known their own boundaries

done better in school

emotionally bonded better

been healthier

said no more easily

had less fear and dependency

had fewer pregnancies

avoided relationships less

While incest may have substantially influenced a survivor's life, she has the power to improve and change her self-concept. In the following comment, one respondent shares her hope:

In the nine months since I started counseling, I've had more hope than ever before in my life that the pain I've felt somewhere inside all the time, and the frustration I've felt at being socially inadequate, could go away. I didn't know why I hurt so much or handled life in general so poorly, why I seemed so weak, but I thought I was made that way—a big mistake on God's part. Now I see the cause/effect, and I see myself feeling less depressed all the time, and I'm beginning to feel like an adult in an adult's world instead of like a weak child overcome by most situations. I've never been happier and I expect it to continue and to learn to cope with hard times (emotionally) in less drastic impulsive ways.

6
Messages about Sexuality and Sex Roles

I ncest profoundly influences what female survivors learn about sex and what they come to believe is expected sex role behavior. By understanding the effects of incest on their sexual socialization, survivors can realize that what they heard was a biased, inaccurate, and limited perspective that essentially had its roots in perpetuating the sexual abuse. While no one can erase the past, it is possible with this knowledge to break away from the crippling beliefs of the past and to learn to appreciate healthy female sexuality.

Given our culture's secretiveness and discomfort about sexuality, the lack of comprehensive sex education, and the myths from past generations, most teenage girls grow up with a limited sense of what positive female sexuality is all about. Feeling good and secure about themselves sexually is unusual for most teenage girls. Five feelings that commonly prevail are guilt, confusion, fear, isolation, and dependency.

For female victims of incest, the situation is even more pronounced. They tend to experience these same feelings more intensely than most other girls do. They also experience two additional feelings, powerlessness and hopelessness, which are direct results of having been sexually abused. Contending with these two extra feelings along with the five other intensified ones leaves incest victims with a double burden. This dilemma of incest survivors is called the piggyback effect of sexual socialization. Table 6–1 shows the relationship between what most teenage girls feel and what teenage incest victims feel in more detail.

Powerlessness for the female incest victim means that she views sexuality as something over which she has no control. Sex was learned as an act of physical submission. Because it was coercive, the sexual activity did not permit the victim to develop limit-setting and assertive-

Table 6–1
The Piggyback Effect of Sexual Socialization

Feeling	Concerns for Most Girls	Additional Concerns for Incest Survivors
Confusion	As to how to express and receive physical affection without jeopardizing personal values or social standing	As to whether any physical affection expressed by others, especially men, is intended as sexual
Fear	That they aren't attractive, won't be sought out by boys, and that others will discover that they are self-stimulating, making out on dates, menstruating, etc.	That the perpetrator's demands will continue or escalate; fear of refusing the perpetrator and of what will happen and what people will think if they find out
Guilt	About sexual desires, fantasies, behavior, and self-stimulation	About participation in the incest and why they didn't stop it before
Isolation	From others in their inability to share sexual feelings, experiences, and thoughts	From others in the secret of incest
Dependency	On boyfriends, parents, doctors, and teachers for information about their own bodies and about which sexual behaviors and feelings are acceptable	On the perpetrator as critical to providing for the family's welfare. Participation in sex is seen as necessary to ensure family survival.
Powerlessness		In their ability to stop the incest
Hopelessness		That they are doomed to sexual submission; that sex will always be a negative experience

ness skills. Abuse survivors often feel at a loss as to how to prevent sexual activity from occurring or how to interrupt it once it has begun. Because their self-concepts are poor, they fail to give themselves permission to say no. During sex they feel unable to express their needs when presented with the demands and needs of their partners. Survivors must develop an ability to project to others the belief that they can set limits in relationships. This ability comes from believing that they are worthwhile and have an equal right to decide the path of the relationship.

The following excerpt reveals a survivor's sense of powerlessness about sexuality and her tendency to assume sexual responsibility and blame. After years of feeling socially isolated, this survivor began having positive experiences in a church, which led to her first romantic relationship:

> The members of the church made me feel loved, wanted, and a part of their happy church family. Soon I was practically living at church, and when I wasn't at church or school, I was with church friends. I was really happy to feel loved. They truly liked me. I began singing in church and was praised for my voice. Through church I met a boy. Soon we were boyfriend and girlfriend. He didn't scare me, because I knew he was a person filled with Christ and wouldn't hurt me. But his morals weren't as high as I thought, and soon we were making out at the movies. This scared me and made me feel wonderful at the same time.
>
> I liked being kissed and touched, but I felt guilty for doing so. We did a lot of heavy petting, and then one day he wanted to go all the way. I didn't want to. I told him no, no, no, but he just wouldn't stop. I was scared, and finally he entered me. I can still remember the physical pain. It was horrible. Afterwards, I felt mentally kind of numb, like I wasn't myself anymore. I was physically sore for a couple of days, and of course, I felt guilty for being a sinner.
>
> I thought the Christian thing to do was marry him. At fifteen and a half years old I was engaged. A month before the wedding, I broke our engagement. My mother had found out why I was marrying him and told me I didn't have to marry him just because I had sex with him. I was relieved. I really did love him, but I didn't want to get married. I'm sorry for hurting him. He loved me, and I broke his heart.

This same survivor went on to describe her next major relationship five years later.

> I started college in September and began seeing a boy. He would come to my dorm room every day and we would get into deep, intellectual, heavy discussions. This wasn't very romantic! I started to fall in love with this person, who was gentle, kind, and unlike any other person I'd ever met. Our relationship was not at all physical. One day he told me that he had to have sex. I told him I wouldn't have sex until I was married, and he told me he would find someone else to have sex with. This frightened me because I had grown dependent on

him. So again I committed the act of sex, which always made me feel guilty. But this time I was in control of the situation. I knew that what I was about to do was wrong and that it would physically hurt. So I had sex with only one thing in mind, to fulfill his needs and keep from losing him. But in doing this, I had to give up my religious beliefs. There was no way I could believe in God and Christianity while doing something that I knew was a sin.

In the second relationship, the survivor felt powerless to balance her own needs for love with her partner's desire for sexual interaction. The control she spoke of was not control of the situation but rather of her decision. She made a conscious choice to exploit herself. Sex was not at all positive. It was physically painful; she was engaging in it only for another's pleasure; and she compromised her religious beliefs and self-esteem.

The feeling of hopelessness reflects the sense that somehow the events of the past will forever predict the events of the future. Survivors may have made the assumption that sexual relating means being exploited, humiliated, and overwhelmed. Here again, the learned victim role from the abuse is evident. There may have been years of abuse, during which the victims hoped and prayed it would stop but it didn't. Past hopes that things would change went unfulfilled for too long, and hope itself became a disappointing experience. Survivors may acquire a fear that they will fail if they ever attempt to change. As one adult survivor wrote:

> I find myself angry at filling out the [sexuality] questionnaire and would prefer not to think of myself as a sexual person at all. I think that because sex and violence were barely distinguishable in my life, I will always be alone and isolated from intimate relationships. I think of sex as a defeat.

Incest survivors have been robbed of the opportunity to experiment with their own sexual feelings in ways that evolve naturally. Self-stimulation and self-exploration were often hindered by the abuse or have become charged with images reminiscent of interactions with perpetrators. Unlike girls raised in families in which sexual boundaries were clearly maintained, victims of incest never got to experiment with expressing their sexual energies on males who could not be seduced. Many survivors did not get to experience hugging and kissing their grandfather, uncle, or father freely and sensually, without any adult sexual overtones present. And many survivors didn't get to experience these males setting limits on their children's touch to avoid sexual arousal. Consequently, many survivors do not know how to initiate sexual behavior based on their own sexual feelings or how to pace sexual contact so that they remain at ease with it or how to stop sexual contact when they feel it is inappropriate.

The basic sex role learned by survivors is that of submissiveness. Their partner's needs are allowed to dominate. This appears to be true for survivors both in same-sex and opposite-sex relationships. Incest teaches victims a self-defeating way to relate to a sexual partner: "I am there for the other person, I am obligated, my feelings don't matter, my enjoyment doesn't matter."

The female victim's sex role corresponds with sex role stereotyping, which is limiting and unbalanced. Male sexual abusers may hold to some very rigid and clearly sexist ideas. For instance, offenders may believe that within the context of the family, women and children are essentially the property of men. A woman's importance in life is viewed as less than a man's. Men are seen as having certain privileges because they are males or because they bring home the paycheck. Women's needs and feelings are seen as subordinate to the male's needs and desires. Women's worth is determined by how well they support and satisfy their men. Children, especially female children, are viewed as extensions of their mothers, with responsibilities to respect the male authority figure. Within this belief system, male authority figures feel justified in using fear, intimidation, and even physical abuse to secure the submission of other family members. This stereotyping establishes a climate in which male domination can go unchecked. Survivors are sometimes amazed to discover that male-female relationships can be based on mutual respect and equality.

Many survivors may have learned myths about the male sex drive. Common myths are that men's desires are more important than women's desires and that once a man feels sexual he must act on his feelings or something terrible will happen to him. These misconceptions leave the survivor feeling that men are sexually wild animals who are out of control. This impression in turn is reinforced by the sexual offender's out-of-control behavior. Survivors often feel it is their obligation to satisfy these overwhelming sexual urges and that if they don't, they will be responsible for the terrible discomfort the male will then experience. A teen survivor said, "I heard that if a man wants sex, you're just supposed to lie back and spread your legs." It's as if men are like cows that require milking on a regular basis or their udders will burst. The truth is that the male sex drive is no greater than the female sex drive; nothing bad will happen if sexual urges aren't acted upon; and the satisfying of sexual feelings is the sole responsibility of the person experiencing them. When a consenting partner is not available, masturbation and abstinence are choices men can and do make.

Another commonly distorted view of sex role differences is the belief that a man can justify having sex with his child or stepchild if his wife refuses or isn't available. In this distortion, female family members are seen as responsible for meeting the needs of male family members. To the offender, going outside the family to get sexual needs met may be seen as less desirable and may represent a failure of the family. The offender may erroneously feel that he is being virtuous by keeping his sexual activity inside the family.

One teen survivor told her story:

> My mom was never home. She worked nights, which was a perfect opportunity. She's worked nights since I can remember, and that's when he started, because she wasn't ever home. I'd ask him why he was doing it and he'd tell me he did it because my mom wasn't home to do it. I'd tell him that just because my mom wasn't there didn't make it *my* responsibility, but he'd tell me that I was the girl of the house. I knew that wasn't fair, but I'd have to do it anyway.

Many female incest survivors have such a strong belief in the inequality of male-female roles that it is difficult for them to entertain the idea that the roles can be otherwise. Some survivors appear to have lost the motivation required to make these roles more equal and to have accepted exploitation instead.

Teen survivors often express fairly pessimistic views of what it means to be female. Many have seen their mothers act submissively in relation to men. In many cases their mothers were emotionally and/or financially dependent on men and were afraid to assert themselves for fear that family survival would be jeopardized. Some survivors expressed a lack of respect for their mothers because they did not take their daughters seriously when they disclosed the incest or when obvious indicators of abuse were present. One teen recalled that during bath time at age four she very clearly told her mother, "He made me put it in my mouth." The mother was startled and yet remained silent. She was living with a boyfriend, who was supporting her and her three children—the natural father had committed suicide one year earlier. An incest survivor herself, she felt paralyzed by the information and forced herself to ignore it, hoping it wasn't true. The message to the daughter was that her needs were less important than the preservation of the male's role in the family.

Incest survivors are particularly vulnerable to the repercussions of our culture's sexual double standard. According to the double standard, the male's social status increases with sexual contacts, while the female's social status decreases. We have only to look at our language to see how this message gets conveyed. Females who engage in frequent sex are given socially derogatory labels, such as tramp, whore, and loose woman. Males are given such labels as stud, jock, and Casanova. Females who lose their virginity are "dirty," males are "experienced." There is one standard for males and another for females concerning the same behavior. Thus, the double standard serves to reinforce survivors' beliefs in male-female role distinctions and makes it more difficult to view themselves as equal with men. To a girl who has not been sexually victimized, male privilege may be an irritating nuisance to be overcome, one that requires her to be assertive. To the girl who has been sexually victimized by a male, male privilege is experienced as a fact of life.

Victims receive distorted messages about love and sex. Given the coercive dynamics of incest, many survivors have assumed that in order to get love they must have sex. Sex becomes the key to obtaining closeness, attention, touching, and intimacy. This confusion about love and sex is experienced as truth by the victim and can often lead to self-exploitation. One woman explained that she made poor relationship choices as she attempted to find nurturing.

> I tend to choose a partner who I can continue the abuse pattern with, i.e., who I can't get my needs met by, feeling like I have to be willing to be sexual at all times for the relationship to be "right" or how it should be (in other words, if I need a day or a week or longer off— that *isn't* okay). I'm being sexual in order to get nurturing and attention, which is what I *really* need.

Another adult survivor expressed her dilemma with regard to sex and caring.

> I have always felt obligated to have sex with any male who gives of their time or spends money on me or seems to care about me. I have

felt that since I have been married and even while I was single that I just plain did not have any justification for saying no. Then if I did say no, it was always knowing that if I was pressured in any way by my partner, I would go ahead. Also I would put a lot of pressure on myself to have sex. I felt very selfish and uncaring if I did not show my concern by sex.

Feeling that they must satisfy their partners with sex in order to secure love triggers negative feelings in survivors. "Why aren't I loved for myself?" "Am I prostituting myself for love?" "I hate his/her desire for sex with me—it's a demand." This orientation, which makes sex a prerequisite for love, establishes sex as a chore rather than something engaged in out of a desire to openly express loving feelings. For many victims, sex with the offender was the only experience in which they felt they were being physically cared for or loved. Receiving sexual attention came to represent being loved. Much confusion then resulted. One survivor remarked, "I confuse arousal in violence with love responses." Incest survivors consequently may have difficulty seeing that sexual expression is only one form of showing love and receiving love. Though the offender may have called it love, the sexual experience of incest was not an expression of love because it was motivated by a desire to satisfy personal needs at the expense of the sexual partner's best interests. Many survivors cannot comprehend that when love is truly being expressed sexually, partners will show sensitivity to the survivors' feelings and will not seek to control or dominate. When a survivor feels she does not have to engage in sex to secure her partner's love, it is a sign of personal growth and security with her partner.

Incest offenders are incapable of teaching anything helpful about sex roles and sexuality. Some offenders cling to the distorted belief that by having sex with the victim they are teaching her to be a good lover. The concept of being a "good lover" only reflects the perpetrators' stereotyped idea of females as submissive pleasers. It's accurate to say that offenders do teach much about love and sex to their victims. However, what they teach is their own harmful, distorted misconceptions about love and sex. It's as if offenders see life through a pair of tinted glasses that color experiences with their fantasies, frustrations, and sexual addictions. When they teach about sex and love, they teach only the view they see through the tinted glasses, not an enlightened reality.

Sexual offenders may pride themselves on being authorities on sex when they are not. They often have inaccurate information about sexual functioning and view sex in an immature fashion. In talking about her experience of having oral sex with her stepfather, one teen shared:

> When I was little he'd make me do it, but I didn't have to drink it or have to swallow it. When I got older he made me swallow it. I'd go, "Why?" and he'd go, "This will make your boobs grow bigger." I started reading some books on sex and told him, "It will not make my boobs grow bigger—those are guy hormones." Then when I started to fill out he said, "That's 'cause of all the cock you sucked."

This teen's stepfather had the audacity to state that her female development had been benefited by the incestuous sexual activity.

Incest survivors can learn to cast aside negative residual feelings of guilt, confusion, fear, isolation, dependency, powerlessness, and hopelessness. They can learn to overcome the false, distorted messages they received about love, sex, and sex roles. Obtaining accurate information about sex, defining what love means to them, and breaking free of oppressive sexual stereotypes are important steps survivors can take.

By correcting misconceptions about sexuality and sex roles left over from the abuse, survivors can become confident in their ability to relate in healthy sexual ways. They may eventually feel more confident than their peers who were not molested. Thus a positive type of piggyback effect is possible. Survivors have a very great potential for creating positive sexual experiences and for relating in mutually respectful sex roles.

7
Anxieties about Relationships

S urvivors of sexual abuse are keenly aware of how unpredictable and hurtful other human beings can be. Having been victimized by people whom they had formerly trusted, incest survivors may feel particularly vulnerable or fearful of further abuse. Since trust was broken by other family members who failed to protect the survivors, these experiences may have left survivors wary of any type of relationship with either sex. Survivors may not feel they have the ability to select good friends and partners. Relationship skills such as developing mutual trust, communicating honestly and assertively, and experiencing playful physical affection may be undeveloped and may even seem foreign.

Young victims frequently react to the incest by generalizing individual characteristics of the offender to other people. One girl, after being abused by a grandfather who had a beard, developed a special fear and distrust of older men with beards. Teens in the survivors' groups were very suspicious about being touched by anyone who reminded them of the offender—even when the only similarity was in being male. They expressed a general fear of men (all their offenders had been males). Teens reported having difficulty differentiating between touching that was friendly and caring and touching that might have been intended as a pass. Some survivors expressed feelings of disgust and repulsion at the sight of male bodies. Chest hair, body smell, and mannerisms similar to those of the offender were taken as warning signs, bringing up fear of sexual abuse. Survivors' concerns went beyond the typical anxiety and embarrassment most teen girls feel around men. Their expectations of male behavior and their awareness of their own sexuality in relation to men were different too.

These teens' remarks illustrate their confusion about men:

If I was standing alone in an elevator and a thirty-three-year-old man walked in, I'd be scared that he was just going to rape me or something. I'm scared to death to be in a room alone with a man.

There's a man who was a good friend of our family's. He used to take us to church all the time. I haven't seen him for a long time, but I saw him recently and he gave me a big hug and it just gave me the creeps. He also gave me a kiss on the cheek and I couldn't stand it. It really freaked me.

I know what you mean. A few weeks ago, a guy from church, his wife, and baby came over. My foster parents, my foster sisters, and these people were all in the bedroom talking. This guy and I were the last ones to go in, and as we were going in, he put his arm around my waist and I felt like he was making a pass at me. Then he started asking me if I was ticklish, and I told him no and to get away from me. I didn't really know what to do.

Every time an older man touches you, you think it's some kind of pass, but sometimes it's not. My grandfather always hugs me, but I just couldn't stand it. I did finally get used to it. I thought he molested my mom, but then I found out that he didn't, and I felt safer.

Fear of males generalizes into teens' relationships with their male peers. Here a survivor shares her concerns about boys:

I needed to have a meaningful relationship with anyone. Because of my experiences with sexuality as a child, I was afraid of boys. I was also afraid of my own sexual desires. I was scared to confide in people. So when I had the urge to think sexual thoughts or masturbate, I felt horribly guilty. I thought there was something wrong with me. I tried to repress any sexual feelings I felt. Not being able to trust was also one of my problems in making friends. I didn't like talking about boys, and always clammed up when discussing sex.

In general the fear of boys is not as strong as the fear of men. Many teens expressed confidence in their ability to defend themselves verbally or physically against the unwanted physical attention of their male peers. However, they did consistently report anxiety about whether boys went out with them primarily to get sex from them or because the boys really liked them.

A concern expressed by teen and adult incest survivors is that they might marry someone who would sexually abuse their children. Some women become extremely suspicious of their partners when there is no cause. Others fear involvement with men who fall into high-risk groups, such as partners who will stepparent existing children or men who themselves were victims of early child abuse.[8] While it is important to be aware that these groups are high-risk, this is not reason enough to avoid a particular relationship. Survivors would benefit more from evaluating the personality characteristics and interpersonal skills of a prospective partner. To illustrate, many stepfathers genuinely care for and respect their new children. And many men who were abused as children grow up to be nurturing, supportive adults highly motivated to give their children what they themselves did not receive. Often the fear of repeating abusive family patterns in itself prevents adult survivors of child abuse from ever being abusive. Female survivors reduce the risk of their children being abused when they are assertive in their marriages, feel relaxed and comfortable with sexual matters, and encourage open communication. In addition, survivors can develop their ability to recognize signs of abuse and stop the abuse if it begins to occur.

Anxieties about future and current relationships can be reduced when survivors learn better how to distinguish abusers from nonabusers. Generalizing about men or women and feeling helpless need to be minimized. Taking a closer look at the characteristics of offenders can help survivors gain skills in partner selection and evaluation. Here is a list of characteristics that may be found in offenders. Survivors may want to use the list as an aid in selecting potentially nonabusing partners.

Sexual offenders are more likely to:

1. Need to feel powerful and controlling in relationships. They may see males as dominant over females in sexual relationships.

2. Have been physically or sexually abused as children and have never dealt with the feelings that resulted.

3. Have difficulty in expressing feelings and maintaining emotional relationships with adults.

4. See sex as the primary means to satisfy their general emotional needs.

5. Attribute sexual characteristics to children and see children as sexual objects. Some may enjoy child pornography or make comments about children being sexually enticing.

6. Have poor self-concepts.
7. Display behavior that may reduce inhibitions, such as alcoholism, psychological disturbance, and drug addiction.
8. Exhibit patterns of distorted thinking to avoid responsibility for their behaviors, such as blaming others, rationalizing, minimizing, shifting conversations, and so on.

A survivor can evaluate her choice of current and future partners using this list. The items listed can be seen as red flags, that is, areas that may signal trouble. There are two ways to use the list. One is to look at how many items on the list characterize a specific partner. A person who exhibits seven or eight of the characteristics is clearly a larger risk than someone who has none of them. However, the other way to use the list is to look at how frequent or intense a behavior is. For example, many people have a tendency to blame others. It is important to note whether this is an occasional behavior or is done several times a day by a person who shows no ability to take responsibility for him/herself. Looking at both how many characteristics are present and how often or intensely they are occurring can give one a good idea about the risk of choosing an abuser.

Survivors can help themselves stop abusive relationship patterns when they learn to select partners for whom sexual relating is only one of several ways to make intimate contact. This will give survivors the chance to experience relationships in a positive new light. Commenting on what helped her move beyond the problems that resulted from the incest, a survivor wrote: "I learned to choose my partner. In the past I used to jump into sexual relationships quickly with only the hope of getting what I wanted. That never worked."

Some survivors have difficulty determining whether they are allowing themselves to be abused in a current relationship. The following list can help survivors to determine if they are consistently allowing themselves to sacrifice their own sense of self in order to remain in a relationship.[9]

In this relationship, am I:

disregarding my own intentions?
overlooking behavior that hurts me deeply?
covering up behaviors that I despise?
appearing cheerful when I am hurt?

keeping up appearances to avoid conflicts?

being disrespected repeatedly?

allowing my standards to be compromised?

faulting myself for the relationship's problems?

believing I have no options?

Each yes answer can be interpreted as an indicator that there is a problem in the relationship. Survivors can learn how to be in relationships without falling into these traps, which perpetuate the victim role. If the items on the list characterize a survivor's responses in a current relationship, then the relationship is not one that fosters honest and open communication. It cannot be satisfying until the abusive and self-defeating behaviors stop.

Survivors may approach new relationships with unrealistic ideas and expectations because their early experiences in relationships were built on manipulation and disappointment rather than trust and honesty. From the start survivors may view new relationships in black-and-white terms. One incest therapist described this as an "I want everything, I deserve nothing" approach. A survivor might have high expectations that a partner will rescue her, love her, and take care of her forever. Later, once the excitement from the romance dies down and the realities of hammering out a mutually satisfying relationship set in, a survivor might take the pessimistic stance that the relationship can't possibly work for her at all. Her partner's withdrawing during a disagreement might be immediately interpreted as a rejection of love. She may become upset and angry, then severely depressed. This flip-flop approach sets up the survivor for relationship failure. It can frustrate partners and discourage their interest. A more realistic view would contain a balance between extreme optimism and pessimism, and a more matter-of-fact, less personalized approach to relationship ups and downs.

The most significant step incest survivors can take to protect themselves from further abuse and to create satisfying relationships for themselves is to approach relationships from a position of strong self-esteem. Good self-esteem means feeling important, worthwhile, valuable, and deserving of respect from others. Without good self-esteem, survivors may attract those people for whom exploitation, deception, and manipulation are a way of life. Low self-esteem impairs one's ability to be assertive, to get out of potentially harmful situations, and to balance needs in relationships. If survivors feel unskilled in communicating effectively and resolving relationship disputes, they can learn these skills as adults through classes, books, or counseling. Feeling confident that one has the tools for maintaining healthy relationships promotes high-level self-esteem.

Survivors often doubt their desirability. They worry that partners will judge them for having been sexual before, as if they are "used property." They may feel permanently marked as bad or worthless by the experience of incest. Some mentally torture themselves with such thoughts as "It didn't really happen"; "It was my fault"; "It degraded me and made me different"; "I could have prevented it"; "My only value is sexual"; and "Nobody will ever love me."

Once in positive relationships it may be hard for survivors to believe that they are being loved for themselves. As one woman said, "Sometimes I think I am too needy and too insecure to be really loved—I keep doubting the relationship." Commenting on how she might have been different if she hadn't been an incest victim, another survivor wrote: "I think I would be negotiating relationships instead of avoiding them as I do now. I find myself in a double bind—alone without an intimate relationship and alone in one."

Many survivors worry about how partners will react to them when they disclose they were incest victims. They may fear their partner will reject them, think that they are different, believe they could have prevented it, or wonder if they enjoyed it. Though many survivors worry unnecessarily and their partners respond with understanding and care, the reactions of some partners are similar to survivors' fears. While there is a risk involved in telling a partner about the incest, the negative outcome of the alternative—not telling—must also be considered. In giving advice to other survivors, one woman wrote, "If your partner won't be supportive and learn about incest, get out of the relationship!"

Every incest survivor deserves support from her partner, and she can increase her chances of getting it by presenting herself as a whole, worthwhile person rather than as a permanently damaged woman. A negative response from a partner is best viewed as the partner's problem rather than the survivor's problem. Many partners lack knowledge about incest. Some partners will not know how to respond, and some will respond poorly. Some will learn to adjust and will respond more positively later. Some will not be willing to work through their own issues and responses.

Survivors who feel clear with themselves about the incest can effectively handle the reactions of partners as they come up. For instance, if a partner begins to imply that perhaps a survivor could have prevented the incest from occurring, then the survivor can respond by educating her partner about the offender's manipulations and the feelings she had during the abuse, and about other dynamics of incest. One woman, when she received a reaction of pity from her partner, told him she was hurt by his response and wanted him to know that she really was fine in spite of the early abuse.

Women who have female sexual partners generally reported that their partners reacted to the incest disclosure with support, anger toward the offender, fear, sadness, and love. These reactions were usually well received by the survivors. Problems arose when the partners' responses made them emotionally unavailable to the survivors.

Many male partners responded with similar emotions of support. However, about half of the male partners in our study reportedly expressed disbelief, blame, a lack of understanding, or other unhelpful responses. One woman wrote, "A relationship that does not encourage talking about feelings and letting out secrets triggers my insecurities." This remark reflects a common desire among survivors for relationships in which both partners value sharing feelings.

Many adult female survivors may have trouble establishing close relationships with women. A mother who knew about the incest but did not protect her daughter broke her trust as surely as a father who molested her. This issue may be even stronger for lesbian women who have been incest victims; some have said that they felt recognition of their lesbianism would have come much earlier in life had they not felt such a lack of trust in women as a result of their relationships with their mothers.

Lesbian survivor relationships may have an added problem. Keeping their lesbian lifestyle a secret can remind them of keeping the secret of the incest. Thus even a positive adult relationship may be strained by anxiety and fear of discovery. As one survivor explained:

> A gay lesbian sort of issue is that because we have to live kind of closeted, I have another secret that I have to carry. Sometimes when we're in a social situation and I have to keep the sexual relationship unknown to other people, I can feel stuff. It's like a trigger. There are certain things that can be real difficult for me, where I just want to go out and scream about it. Now it's a real positive thing. Then it was a real negative. But keeping the secret—having that feeling inside that

there's this thing that you would like to have out, that's something I think is different. If you're in a heterosexual relationship and things happen that are good as you're recovering from incest, you can go around and tell people in the office and your friends and your family. You can say I'm really loving George and it's so wonderful. You can go to your family—I mean maybe not everyone, but a lot of people— and say the sexual relationship is good and complete and whole, and you get encouragement and validation for that and for the relation- ship. And for us, all that has to be kept quiet. When there are extra tensions in the relationship because of the incest, we don't have the validation coming from family and the world out there to keep it together. And that hasn't been a problem for us but I've seen that in other lesbian couples. The strain of having to hold the relationship together alone makes you just so much more isolated that to add the incest into it makes it more difficult for those relationships to survive.

Incest survivors can greatly help themselves by choosing to relate to people who are understanding of what they have been through, accepting of who they are now, and responsive to what they need. To accomplish this, survivors must give themselves permission to relate to sensitive, accepting people. This may not feel comfortable at first, as survivors have been used to unequal relationships in which their needs are not met. However, the level of comfort increases with time and will pay enormous benefits in the long run as survivors discover how truly nurturing relationships can be.

8
How Incest Affects Sexuality

Incest appears to strongly influence the subsequent sexual behavior and experiences of many survivors. (See Appendix A for a review of research findings in this area.) This chapter focuses on three major areas in which sexual repercussions are evident. These areas are (1) sexual emergence in early adulthood, (2) sexual orientation and preference, and (3) sexual arousal, response, and satisfaction.

It is important to keep in mind that each woman's sexuality is affected by a variety of influences, such as biological drive, religious training, educational awareness, and social group. These influences can exert themselves powerfully on her sexual development. While a history of sexual abuse *can* constitute the most dramatic influence, conclusions about its strength must be tempered by these other factors. More research is needed to address these differences through specific control group studies.

Sexual Emergence

In the teen years following sexual abuse, survivors often gravitate toward one of two extreme sexual lifestyles. Survivors seem to either become socially and sexually withdrawn from their peers or to plunge into a phase of promiscuous and sometimes self-destructive sexual activity.

The withdrawal response can reflect a survivor's fears about sex, anxieties about partners, and poor self-image. Symptoms of withdrawal include refusing dates, staying socially isolated, pretending that sex doesn't exist, and denying sexual feelings. Survivors may have distorted ideas about what will be expected of them if they go out.

They may imagine that dating will require sexual willingness and responsiveness. They may believe that their date's main focus will be "getting some sex." Survivors may have little trust in their own ability to say no or to protect themselves and may instead want to avoid a situation in which they expect to once again feel overpowered and paralyzed. Some survivors have mentioned that they think their withdrawal from sex is a way in which they try to "buy their way back to heaven." Celibacy may be practiced in an effort to compensate for what they believe was their sin.

The opposite response, that of unusually frequent sexual activity, also reflects the early sexual victimization. Some survivors learned from the incest that their sexual attentions can give them a feeling of special power over men. They may fail to see how superficial this feeling is and how much it reflects a reaction to the powerlessness they experienced earlier in life. Many survivors use sexual promiscuity to prove to themselves that their sexuality is now their own. By "choosing" to sleep with many partners, the survivor attempts to give herself a sense of being in control of her sexuality. This effort to achieve a positive goal can backfire, however, because of the lack of true satisfaction generally provided by it. Indiscriminate sexual activity may have other repercussions as well, such as unwanted pregnancies, abortions, venereal disease, loss of social respect, and exploitation, all of which impact negatively on self-esteem.

Frequent sexual activity can be a form of intentionally self-destructive behavior on the part of the survivor. She may feel guilty for the incest and try to punish herself through self-degrading activities. Comments such as "This is all that I'm good for" and "I'm a whore anyway, so why not?" reflect this attitude. Some survivors actually become prostitutes. This may result when sexual abuse victims run away from home to escape the offender. They may turn to prostitution as a means of supporting themselves. Their need for affection and their limited image of themselves as sexual objects make them prime targets for people who wish to sexually exploit them. In an article written in 1978, James and Meyerding stated that 65 percent of the prostitutes they studied had had a history of forced negative sexual experiences.[10] Another study found 80 percent of prostitutes to have been sexually abused in childhood.[11]

Early sexual abuse appears to create a disruption in the normal dating patterns of adolescence. Teen survivors commonly allude to confusion about the normal sequence of dating and sexual behavior.

Such questions arise as whether to kiss on the first date, at what point it is appropriate to hold hands, and at what stage sexual contact should enter into the relationship. An example of this confusion was provided by a girl who had been sexually abused by her stepfather. He repeatedly told her that boys would not like her unless she made out with them and had sex with them. At age twelve she was at a party and met a fifteen-year-old boy. They began making out.

> I was frenching him, just making out, and he was blown away that a twelve-year-old would know how to do all this stuff. He didn't want to stop. For six months after that he was calling me every day. I'd tell him to get off the phone. I didn't want to talk to him. It was weird. The guy was a total jerk.

Having experienced adult forms of sexual contact at an early age, incest victims run the risk of unknowingly acting in sexually inappropriate ways with their peers. When this problem is combined with the burden of misinformation from offenders about the part sex plays in a relationship, it is understandable that confusions and fears about dating persist. Age-inappropriate sexual expression can result in a teen survivor acquiring a social reputation for being "loose." This hurtful labeling may encourage her to think of herself as cheap.

Confusion about dating appears to persist over time. Over half the adult incest survivors in our study reported that they frequently experience confusion over the normal sequence of dating and sexual behavior. It can be helpful for survivors to discuss what constitutes appropriate dating behavior with other survivors or with a therapist (see appendix C for worksheet).

In an attempt to escape anxieties about dating and sexual interactions, some survivors regularly use drugs and alcohol, which reduce inhibitions and allow them to "space out" from what is happening. Female alcoholics have often been incest victims. For a number of alcoholic and drug-addicted incest survivors, sober sexual experiences are rare. While temporarily drowning out the discomfort engendered by intimate physical contact, these methods reinforce feelings of victimization, of being out of control, and of being exploited by others. Healthy social development is arrested when relating depends on being in an altered state of consciousness. Chemically induced highs really create withdrawal from rather than connection to other people.

A number of survivors reported having relatively little trouble with dating and premarital sexual experiences. Yet many of these same women report that once married, the sexual feelings plummeted and they began to feel trapped into being sexual. The real or imagined demands of their mates for sexual contact reminded them of the sexual obligation of incest.

Sexual Orientation and Preference

Incest, which is such a profoundly upsetting experience, seems to bring with it the possibility of influencing sexual preference in many different ways. For instance, studies of boys who were sexually victimized by men do indicate that a high percentage of them relate homosexually as adults.[12] The reasons for this are speculative. Perhaps sexual arousal becomes linked with visual images of aroused men, and is reinforced by the pleasurable sensation of orgasm.

Of the twelve women in our study who had sexual relations with other women, about half felt strongly that the incest had no bearing on their sexual preference. The other half felt the incest *was* related to their choice of same-sex partners. We speculate that these women represent two different groups. The first group of women are lesbians who also happen to be incest survivors. They would have been lesbian with or without the incest experience. The other group of women may be basically heterosexual or bisexual and have been open to experimentation with female partners as part of their healing process. For them, the incest had an impact on their choices. All the women in this second group in our study had experienced both male and female partners. One women in this group said, "My relationships with women were influenced by the incest. I was looking for an equal instead of someone dominating me."

There are many reasons why a heterosexual female survivor might choose female partners. Female partners may be less pressuring than males for sexual contact, and more understanding and supportive of the survivor's anxieties about sex. Some survivors may feel safer and more comfortable with females because their bodies lack many of the reminders of the abuse, such as a penis, semen, and body hair, and because their voices do not remind them of the low voice of the offender. Resolving incest issues can lead these women to overcome their old fears and can give them the option of relating to men, sometimes much to the dismay of their woman-oriented friends. For these women, the incest may have blocked the recognition of their underlying heterosexual orientation.

In contrast, women who are lesbian from early childhood may find that the incest—forced sexual contact with males—blocks their awareness of their preference for female partners. Anger at women, encouraged by anger at a mother who failed to protect, can also block recognition of attraction to women. These women may have spent years assuming they were heterosexual. One survivor hypothesized how she would have been different had she not been a victim of incest.

> I would not have been promiscuous with men. I would not associate pain with sexual pleasure. I would not have abusive sexual fantasies. I would have realized I'm a lesbian earlier.

Further illustration is given by another survivor in this poignant story:

> The incest really restricted how I conceived of my sexuality because I had never even masturbated. I hated my body. I just hated it. And so I was simply nonsexual most of my life. The incest blocked my sexuality. In looking back now, I think if I hadn't been abused and really believed that I was my father's property, my sexual preference for women would have started developing when I was in junior high. I was really close to another girl, who I know to be lesbian. I had feelings toward other women too when I was in junior high, but I didn't spend much time thinking about it. I wanted to be asexual completely, so any feelings that I had like that I pushed away. Whether they were for women or men, I just did not want anyone close to me.
>
> After I got out of my home—well, actually, after my father left the home (he was the perpetrator)—I hardly ever dated. I just became resolved that I'd be single—celibate. That didn't bother me, because I put all my efforts into my career and I didn't care. I didn't have very many close friends at all. I was very isolated. I felt safest that way. It wasn't until I was twenty-seven, I think, that I began going out. I just had a few friends who were men. They were good relationships, but I never allowed them to become sexual relationships. When men would approach me I would get very cold. But with John I really liked him a lot. I loved him, but it wasn't the same kind of love that I have with Sharon. I didn't know that at the time. I had no awareness that I was lesbian. John and I lived together for about six months, I would say, and I found that the sexual side of the relationship was extremely difficult for me, and I think part of that is because I'm

lesbian and I didn't know that at the time, but part of it was definitely incest-related. When he would be really affectionate with me, or when we would have sex, I would almost always get sick to my stomach, and I would go to the bathroom after I thought he was relaxed, and I usually threw up. There were maybe one or two times that I felt I enjoyed sex with him. Most of the time I didn't feel anything. I never had an orgasm.

I knew that a lot of the problem was stuff that had gone on with my dad, and I never felt that I could really share with John the extent of the abuse that I had. He never really wanted to know. He knew that there had been a lot of physical abuse in my family. He was real slow and gentle in approaching me, and whenever I would say anything, he would always respect that. But I really didn't share very much with him, and he also didn't really want to know—he never asked me about it. So it was just kind of a hidden, unspoken thing that caused a lot of problems there. I think, for me, I didn't have any conscious awareness of being lesbian until I had gotten through a lot of work on the incest. I rarely had sexual fantasies before I found I was lesbian. Once I realized I was woman-oriented, I began to fantasize more. Now I do think about sex. I never did that with John. It was something that I didn't really like. But I think there may be people who are gay because of environmental factors—could perhaps go either way, but the environment pushes them. And then I think there are people for whom it's biological. My feeling is that I was lesbian from the time I was born. In thinking back through my life I know that I was always much closer with my friends who were women. I remember physical contact with women that was really pleasurable and enjoyable, and that stayed—left an impression. But I didn't categorize it as sexual or erotic. I think it was, but I wouldn't admit that it was then.

Once I found John I felt this was what I was supposed to do— marry him and have a family. The early association that sex is with a man made it difficult for me to find where I should be. I think there would be some lesbians who because of the abuse really rebelled and found it very easy to find women then. But I'm just saying that for me it was blocked.

Sharon and I had been really close friends, and then just all of a sudden I was in love with her. I was freed up enough from dealing with the incest to recognize my sexuality. But for me, the two things were really closely related. Until I had really dealt with that and been freed, I didn't have any awareness of my own sexual preference. I'd been so dominated by my father. So brainwashed to think that I was male property. I just had no conception of looking to women for a sexual relationship. Even though from the time I was about eighteen, I knew . . . I didn't know before then . . . but I knew from eighteen on that there were women who were homosexual. But I didn't have any awareness of my own orientation.

Many questions are raised in this area of sexual orientation and preference. How do biological, social, and environmental factors influence sexual orientation? Is everyone bisexual to begin with? How does incest impact preference? What is the effect of female offenders? What messages are given to children molested by both sexes? Future research may help provide the answers.

Sexual Arousal, Response, and Satisfaction

Incest can cause problems in sexual functioning that feel as if they have always existed or that slowly surface later in the survivor's life. Survivors tend to experience more sexual problems than women who are not abused (the major areas of sexual problems found in our study are listed in appendix B). Sexual problems may be very frustrating both to the survivor herself and to her partner. As one survivor explained:

> In retrospect, I can see how the incest experiences of over thirty years ago still govern and pattern my sexuality. I have a very diminished sexual appetite, with little curiosity or interest. It is difficult for me to anticipate, enjoy, express, and receive love in a sexual, physical form. A wall of avoidance, fear, and dread has replaced any thrill or urge or anticipation I have known at other times in my life. For some reason, not being in a secure, committed relationship made it easier to be sexual. Now it's as though a part of my life energy has dulled and become inaccessible to me. I feel very out of touch with my body sensually. Feelings of sexiness, attractiveness, and physical competence are only memories. Fatigue and lethargy have come to mask the loss of my sexuality. I feel "bad" and "guilty" for no longer being the exciting, fulfilling lover I once was. Rather, I feel sad and old and withered sexually and romantically.

Lack of sexual desire is a common complaint of incest survivors. It appears related to an array of problems associated with arousal. Regardless of whether survivors felt pain, pleasure, or numbness during the actual physical experience of the incest, most of them seem to identify sexual arousal with the feelings they were having during the abuse. At the time of the incest their concept of sexuality and their biological response to sexual stimulation became associated with their negative feelings toward the abuse. Consequently, if survivors felt helplessness, anger, or guilt at the time of the abuse, they may later find these same feelings surfacing as soon as they begin to engage in sexual behavior.

Women in our study reported associating several feelings with the sexual experience. These included helplessness, disgust, anger, loss of control, guilt, and hate. This negative conditioning is very strong in survivors because the sexual abuse usually constituted their first experience with overt sexual stimulation, and their negative feelings were reinforced through the repetition of the sexual abuse.

For people who have not experienced sexual abuse, an analogy may be helpful for gaining an understanding of this conditioning process. Suppose you were encouraged to play on a softball team when you were young. During your first game, you were suddenly hit in the face by a thrown bat and it smashed your nose. At the time you may have felt scared, helpless, angry, and hurt. After that, softball may have had a different meaning. Perhaps it was no longer seen as a safe sport; thinking of it or playing it may have become associated with anxious feelings. You may even have developed a fear of bats and avoided being near them. Later it might be hard to separate your feelings about the injury from your feelings about the game. The negative association might have become so strong that new experiences would be required to change your response to a positive one.

A similar negative association with sexuality occurs through incest. As one woman wrote, "It's difficult to enjoy stimulation to my genital area when that stimulation vividly reminds me of a previous offensive experience." Some women who were violently and sadistically assaulted during the abuse later report that sexual arousal has become paired with violent sexual behavior. Since they may have experienced getting sexually turned on during the violence, they learned to associate the two. A twenty-six-year-old woman was subjected to fondling, intercourse, and oral sex for five years by her brother and was tortured, tied up, locked in a small room, and raped with objects. She said:

> Many women, including me, are attracted to what happened and get very aroused with a repeat. Why do you think bondage, S/M, etc.

are so popular? It's a repeat of incest—this is how I react. Loving gentle sex is too scary—a repeat of "torture" is arousing, in a very scary way.

Incest creates conflicts and confusions about sex. Since sexual abuse, family betrayal of trust, and sexuality got strongly intertwined in childhood experiences, it's hard to look back and comfortably separate each part so that sex can be experienced in a new light. Yet this is the challenge to the survivor and one that deserves plenty of time. Another survivor, who had been in therapy for three years, described how she has slowly been able to begin experiencing sexual activity without the previous feelings of anger, helplessness, and disgust. She said:

> I can feel overwhelmed with the hurt and confusion. I can feel how painful it was to enjoy something that was mentally and emotionally repugnant. The conflict in feelings may come over me, [yet recently] I have found my sexuality surprisingly intact.

Lack of pleasure in sex can also come from placing primary importance on the partner's experience. Most survivors learned to do this during the sexual abuse. To her own detriment, a woman may primarily focus on her present partner and ask herself, "Am I doing it right? Am I giving my partner what is desired?" However, in order to obtain more sexual arousal and enjoyment, the survivor needs to focus primarily on her own experience during sex. Helpful thoughts might be, "I am relaxed. I can allow myself to enjoy this sexual contact. What can I do or ask for to receive more enjoyment?"

Incest survivors report a phenomenon of having flashbacks or sudden images of the feelings, sights, smells, sounds, or other reminders of the incest. Like an uncontrollable nightmare, a flashback can instantly transport the survivor back in time, so that she mentally reexperiences the abuse. Sensations like pain and nausea may be felt again. The flashback may result in physiologically tightening up and thus losing any arousal that may have been present. Flashbacks can occur several times in one sexual encounter or may occur only once in a while. They can be a major distractor from the positive experience of current sexuality. They can also occur in stressful, nonsexual situations when the survivor least expects them. While flashbacks may be brought on by too much stress, increased relaxation may also leave a survivor feeling unprotected. As one survivor explained:

To be sexual, I have to work at relaxation. If I relax so that I can have an orgasm, sometimes stuff (like anger and old fears) that's been fermenting about the incest will go WHOOM and will come up, and then everything falls apart and I get real upset or I have a flashback or I'll cry or something. And that will interfere with the sex that was initiated between us.

Thoughts and sensations that occur naturally during sex—such as heavy breathing, the smell of sweat, moaning sounds, and sensual touching—may trigger a flashback to the incest. While for other adults these sounds, smells, and forms of touching might enhance sexual feeling, they may temporarily distract and possibly immobilize the sexual response of an incest survivor.

A huge variety of triggers exists. Almost anything can become a trigger if it is associated with incest; what constitutes a trigger is based on each woman's individual sexual experience. Table 8–1 lists a

Table 8–1
Triggers-Stimuli Associated with Incest Memories

1. Smells
    Cigarette smoke
    Alcohol
    Sweat
    Dust
    Strong coffee
	5. Events
	    Being in certain sexual positions
	    Dreams
	    Being physically moved by
	       someone

2. Sounds
    Music
    Tone of voice
    Spoken words
	6. Sensations
	    Sexual arousal
	    Sexual responses
	    Touching
	    Feeling dirty

3. Times
    Nighttime
    Waking up
    Seasons
    Holidays
    Evening at home
	7. Sights
	    Water
	    Men
	    Old men
	    Plaid shirts
	    Clothes
	    Gray hair
	    Facial characteristics
	    Large people
	    Protruding lower lip

4. Places
    Driving on certain roads
    Darkness
    Bathrooms
    Unfamiliar places
    Tents
    Surroundings reminiscent of place
       where incest occurred
	8. Interpersonal Dynamics
	    Personality
	    Attitude
	    Gestures of caring

number of things that triggered memories of the incest for the women in our study.

When asked to comment on what she viewed as sexual problems specific to incest survivors, one respondent wrote:

> Having the idea that you aren't the person in your body (feeling your body may be on the bed but the rest of you melts into the wall), your body functions like a machine, you are unable to discriminate sexual likes from dislikes (this is like being unable to taste/experience the difference between curried rice and spinach; there are no sex "taste buds"), feeling you are powerless, you are unable to relax major body muscles (not necessarily genitalia), you are hypersensitive to relationship dynamics, you tend to second-guess the other person, you experience changes in body maturity (when you let go your body may feel like it's age ten, eight or two, short legs, no boobs, no pubic hair—this can make for some *bizarre* interactions), and you have confused ideas of your size in relation to your partner's size.

Problems with becoming aroused, painful intercourse, lack of orgasm in masturbation, and lack of orgasm with a partner inhibit sexual satisfaction. Those survivors who are orgasmic often report that their orgasms are not enjoyable. For most women, masturbation serves to facilitate the learning process of becoming orgasmic. But for the survivor, self-stimulation may be an unpleasant reminder of sexual feelings from the incest and consequently may be either avoided or engaged in with a detached attitude.

Incest is sexual, and so by its very nature it has sexual repercussions for its victims. These repercussions can function as sexual disabilities, blocking healthy expression and enjoyment of sex. However, the sexual problems resulting from early abuse need not be permanent. Survivors can come to realize that, if they are motivated and have support, they can make changes.

9
How Survivors Can Help Themselves

I know the devastation of incest can be overcome. Hundreds of my
patients have done it. I did it. So can others.

— Susan Forward
Betrayal of Innocence

Many survivors have serious reservations about their ability to
successfully overcome the sexual repercussions of incest.
They doubt that they can resolve sexual problems, lose
their fear of sex, stop feeling guilty about sex, and learn to control the
negative feelings they have about sex. While this attitude of discour-
agement may reflect the learned hopelessness that resulted from early
victimization, it also stems from an awareness of how significantly survivors feel their sexuality was affected. Influences from incest tend to
be deeply ingrained and are often unconscious. They are multidimen-
sional and affect sexual attitudes, beliefs, behaviors, associations, and
self-concept. Thus, trying to overcome the sexual repercussions of incest can feel much like wrestling with an octopus. Unless you have a
sense of what you are doing, and know how to reduce the octopus to
the size of a crab, it's easy to get exhausted and give up hope.

Sexual problems that resulted from incest do not go away by themselves. Treating them successfully requires an effective, well-focused
effort that addresses the ingrained results of the abuse. This is why
seeking outside professional help in the form of psychotherapy is
recommended (see chapter 11). Yet many survivors either do not feel
ready for or currently have no access to incest and sex therapy. They
want to be given basic ideas that they can start using right away to help
themselves.

Whether or not they are currently involved in an intimate relationship, survivors can help themselves make positive changes in the sexual area of their lives. So many times survivors become stuck in old,
self-defeating patterns that reinforce unsatisfying sexual experiences.
By following the suggestions in this chapter, survivors will be using a
well-directed approach to begin resolving sexual concerns.

Survivors can learn on their own to feel better about their bodies and better about the expression of their sexual energy. Since survivors experienced their bodies as objects manipulated for another's benefit, they were denied a comfortable opportunity to develop ownership and control over their bodies and the expression of their sexual energy.

As adults, survivors can provide themselves with new experiences to learn some of what they missed. General body acceptance can be facilitated when survivors take the time to privately look at themselves nude in a full-length mirror, massage their skin, or slowly rub lotion on themselves. Looking at their genital area with a mirror, naming all the sexual parts, and touching the sexual parts to explore the different sensations are all good ways to extend the sense of ownership to more sexual areas. Self-stimulation of sexual parts, which may or may not lead to orgasm, can enable survivors to feel that their sexuality exists primarily for themselves. They can also learn more about what they find sexually satisfying—information critical to further sexual satisfaction with a partner. Women who are comfortable with their bodies and with self-stimulation tend to be more easily orgasmic and generally more satisfied in sexual relationships. These exercises should be done when a woman is alone, and she should move through them at her own pace. This will allow her to fully experience being in control of the experience, which is very important. Body image does not change quickly, but it can change. The exercises become more comfortable with practice, and they are most effective when repeated over time.

Survivors can create a foundation for positive future sexual relationships by learning how to distinguish caring touch from exploitive touch. Caring touch respects the receiver's feelings and gives the receiver room to say no at any time. Exploitive touch is primarily for the benefit of the toucher and tends to deny or discredit the withdrawal of the receiver. Nonsexual relationships that involve an exchange of touch through hand-holding, hugs, friendly kisses, and physical closeness can be very healing to incest survivors and can help them establish trust and a sense of physical control. In a teen group, one survivor shared how important her foster father has been in teaching her about caring touch from a man.

> I'm finding that in my foster home I'm getting the love that I never got from my father. I had thought that affection from fathers was them lusting after my body. Since I was four years old, which is when

my mom married my stepdad, what I remember is him going after my body and just wanting my body. Now my foster father kisses me good night or kisses me goodbye, and he's showing me love in a secure way and the way in which a father should show love. He's really good about it. He told me that if he ever did anything that made me uncomfortable, like hugging me or something, I should just say so and he would find it really understandable. I'm tempted to call him Dad because I never had a dad who was nice like that. He was the one who said I couldn't kiss my boyfriend, but he did that to protect me. He said he knew I could just go out and do whatever I felt like, but he told me that it was because he loved me, and loved me as much as any of his daughters, that he didn't want me to do certain things. He shows me the same kinds of things that he shows any of the other kids in his home.

Single survivors may want to develop social and assertiveness skills before pursuing an intimate relationship. They may find it helpful first to establish friendships with people they are sexually attracted to before acting on those sexual feelings. Having several months in which to get to know and trust a partner, express feelings, and learn to touch in a slow, safe, pleasant way, can give survivors the time they need to relax about sex and view it as one possible choice on a continuum of options for loving physical expression.

Based on informaton and advice provided by survivors themselves, the following "bill of rights" can serve as a reference for survivors in developing assertive attitudes and behaviors regarding sex.

Bill of Sexual Rights

1. I have a right to own my own body.
2. I have a right to my own feelings, beliefs, opinions, and perceptions.
3. I have a right to trust my own values about sexual contact.
4. I have a right to set my own sexual limits.
5. I have a right to say no.
6. I have a right to say yes.
7. I have a right to experience sexual pleasure.
8. I have a right to be sexually assertive.
9. I have a right to be the initiator in a sexual relationship.
10. I have a right to be in control of my sexual experience.

11. I have a right to have a loving partner.
12. I have a right to my sexual preferences.
13. I have a right to have a partner who respects me, understands me, and is willing to communicate with me.
14. I have a right to talk to my partner about the incest.
15. I have a right to ask questions.
16. I have a right to receive accurate sexual information.

A good exercise for a survivor to do on her own is to read through the above bill of rights and make a note by each right that she feels she has not incorporated in her life. Next, she can explore changing her thoughts to include the rights that she would like to accept. Thoughts are like cassette tapes playing on the metaphorical tape deck of one's mind. An old thought can be challenged and erased and a new thought can be played repeatedly until it becomes a new belief. For instance, a survivor may be having trouble with the seventh item on the Bill of Sexual Rights: "I have a right to experience sexual pleasure." She can challenge her belief by asking, "Why don't I feel I have that right? What am I afraid of if I assume that right?" She can visualize herself having the right and imagine how much better she might feel.

By asserting their rights, survivors of incest can begin to see sex in a new way, that is, not as something forced but as something healthy that is freely chosen. Survivors frequently commented about the importance of saying no when they either knew they didn't want sex or when they were unsure. An important point is that a person cannot really say yes to sex unless she/he can also fully say no to it *at any time,* even after sexual activity has begun. Claiming the right to say no is a step toward leaving the victim role behind and developing stronger self-esteem.

Women in our study shared those things they have done that have helped to resolve sexual issues. These included reading and learning about incest; learning how to relax, how to acquire self-confidence, and how to be assertive; reading about sex, relationships, and self-esteem; talking with their partner and sharing what was uncomfortable about sex; learning to be vulnerable; learning how to choose a partner; stopping abusive sexual patterns; taking a "vacation from sex" by becoming celibate for a while; becoming monogamous; learning to relate emotionally with a partner; learning to be patient and to take time; developing a clear sense of sexual boundaries and limits (what they would and wouldn't do, what was needed from a partner); and learning to recognize and allow anger.

Asked what advice they would give to other incest survivors, women made the following insightful comments:

> Don't ever feel guilty about the acting out behavior in your past—such as promiscuity, pregnancies, or abortions.

> Say no until you really want to say yes. Share the feelings that come up with your partner when they come up or as soon as you can. Explore your own body. Learn to please yourself and teach your partner. Allow yourself to be pleased, to receive, to be vulnerable.

> Talk about sex, read about it, write about it—if it's your time. Don't force the river. It's all waiting for you whenever you're ready.

> Talk openly about sex and incest, and remember they're different.

> Concentrate on body touch and safety—not sexual pleasure. Say no especially when you are feeling maybe.

Sometimes a heterosexual survivor is anxious about entering a relationship with a male because men frighten or intimidate her. There is a simple exercise she can do to help overcome this. It's called "putting on blinders." Blinders are the black covers that horses wear to prevent them from seeing sideways. The survivor imagines she is wearing blinders that prevent her from seeing that she is a female. She thus relates as a genderless person, neither female nor male. The man is also imagined as a genderless person. The survivor relates to his eyes, to what he is saying, to his personality, and so forth, not to his maleness and what maleness has previously meant to her. This technique can allow the survivor to overcome initial anxiety and assert her strength in developing a relationship.

Once they have become involved in a relationship and are sexually active, survivors may experience flashbacks to the abuse while they are having sex. Here are some suggestions for survivors for how to cope with flashbacks. First, survivors can identify the triggers that tend to remind them of the abuser and the abusive sexual activity. Once these triggers have been identified, exposure to them can be minimized. For example, cigarette smoke and alcohol may trigger flashbacks for one survivor. She might then establish as a condition for being sexual that she and her partner not consume alcohol or smoke cigarettes before sex. If one or both of them have done either of these, steps can be taken before sex to minimize the effects, such as brushing teeth or using a mouth freshener. Survivors may choose to let their partners know about their triggers so that the two of them can work as a team to find solutions.

Some triggers, such as moaning, sweat, sexual smells, and heavy breathing, present a different challenge, since they cannot realistically be avoided during sex. A request to breathe lightly and to stop sweating will just not be well received by even the most understanding partner! In these situations, some preventive measures may be taken, such as bathing before sex or using an enjoyable perfume that establishes a new smell. Other options for reducing triggers include making love someplace other than a bedroom, changing the time of day for sexual activity, or changing the position for making love to one in which the survivor is more dominant.

In the following excerpts, a survivor describes how she was able to minimize disturbing feelings that would arise around sexual activity by changing the place where intimate contact took place, and how she used cleansing to help her break the old associations with sex as "dirty."

We couldn't start making love in the bed. When we started the sexual contact, it was in the living room, a safer place for me. And I found the first time we went to bed together we went to the ocean, so we weren't really at home, and that was okay. But then when we came back, the next time we went to bed was in my apartment. I had a flashback. Then I found it very threatening when I was in bed. That was real difficult for me, to be in a bed. So that was something else. Though I don't know if we thought about it consciously, it made it easier for me to move into the sexual relationship by being careful about where we were in the house. Definitely not the kitchen. Definitely not the bedroom. Those were the two places for me that were very threatening. The bathroom, for me, was a really safe place. And we kind of played around a lot in the bathroom. We took showers. That was a safe place for me as a child—I could go lock the door. Most of the abuse for me took place in the kitchen and the bedroom. So we'd take a shower together and scrub each other, wash each other's hair, things like that. But if anything sexual was initiated, it was always in the living room. . . . Showering and cleansing bring up good feelings for me. When I have a flashback, or when I've got lots of stuff going on and I'm feeling kind of dirty, I do that. I just allow myself to go in and take a bath every now and then, when I don't need one. Just to feel clean. And it's a physical act that symbolizes a psychological one. Saying, no, I'm now clean. I wash that away.

In the process of reclaiming sexuality as something positive and healthy, women need to remind themselves that the current situation is different from the past. Before they were children, and now they are adults. Their present partners are different from the abusers of the past. Survivors can now trust their own feelings. If sex is uncomfortable or undesired they can speak up and take action. Survivors can develop ways of reminding themselves that now is not the past. Talking during sex to hear their own adult voice and that of their present partner, and reminding themselves where they are and whom they're with can help. Some survivors find they can relax and center themselves by looking around at favorite objects and saying to themselves such statements as "I am big now. I am in control. I am an adult."

The feeling that she can control whether or not sexual interaction takes place as well as the pace of the interaction is a key element in a survivor's sexual healing. Being able to say no to sex at any time includes being able to say no even after sex has begun or is about to be over. The ability to say no with sensitivity to the partner's experience is an important relationship skill. Thus, pushing the partner away abruptly is less desirable than calmly informing him or her and remaining present to hug, calm down, and rest together. Stopping the sexual activity is a way for the survivor to remind herself that she is in control and can say no at any time. Her partner's acceptance of her decision to stop ensures her that she is cared for and respected.

Stopping also provides the survivor with the time needed to refocus on sex from a relaxed perspective, should she and her partner wish to resume overt sexual contact. When possible, it is a good idea for a survivor to indicate to her partner how touching could then be resumed. Perhaps resuming by touching another part of the body or merely slowing down would be a good way to proceed. The process of shifting to a different kind of touching is a way for a survivor to gain control while reinforcing to herself that touching can be a positive experience. One survivor explained:

In my present state and partnership, we each have varying sexual feelings, communicate about them, and act appropriately on them each time. Sometimes old memories and feelings come back and I take time, often with the help of my partner, to separate the present from the past. Often at those times he'll just hold and rock me. That helps.

Once assured that they have the ability to say no and to control the contact comfortably, survivors can slowly explore the option of saying yes willingly and of creating a relaxed setting in which to enjoy sexual expression. Survivors can learn to take an active role in pursuing sexual fulfillment. They can learn to ask comfortably for what they want in lovemaking.

One survivor shared a different approach for overcoming negative feelings that came up during sex. She would challenge herself to be as actively involved as her partner in the sexual activity. She noticed that by bringing herself up to his energy level she could overcome any vulnerable feelings that had begun to surface. She was not just responding to him but was actively matching her activity level with his. As this survivor said, "If you can deaden yourself sexually, then you are powerful enough to drum up your sexual energy at will!"

The ability to laugh about her situation and about sex in general is a good sign that a survivor is on the road to healthy recovery. Developing a sense of humor about sex can reduce anxiety and foster personal change. When sex can be viewed as playful fun among equals, then significant healing has occurred.

10
Survivors and Partners Working Together

The repercussions of incest can hinder the development and expression of intimacy in committed relationships. Often the incest is never identified as the source of a couple's current problems. It may surprise, and depress, survivors to discover that their sexual concerns do not magically disappear once they have found the right partner. In fact, sexual intimacy may become more difficult. The emotional closeness of a committed relationship can be frightening and uncomfortable for survivors, and they may experience feeling obligated to engage in sex.

It is not uncommon for a relationship between a survivor and her partner to become strained in areas of physical intimacy. As a result, both people may begin to emotionally distance and resent each other. This resentment can grow over a long period of time before it is recognized and acknowledged. Unless the couple identifies the problem, resolves negative feelings, and works together to address the real issues, this resentment may eventually destroy the relationship. Separation, divorce, and infidelity are some of the possible negative outcomes.

Often survivors and partners end up in an unfortunate cycle. For example, a female survivor begins to withdraw sexually because of unresolved trust issues and sexual problems from the incest. Her male partner takes this as a personal rejection and stops expressing loving feelings; he may also become angry and sexually demanding. The partner's positive feelings for the survivor start to wane as a result of feeling ignored and alone. The survivor then feels guilty and pressured. She interprets the reactions of the partner as proof that he is unresponsive to her emotional needs. The survivor pulls back emotionally and physically even further. The cycle continues with emotional and physical distance increasing.

Relationships can be weakened by the problems incest brings, if they go unattended, or they can be strengthened in mutually beneficial ways, if the challenges presented by the incest are met by both the survivor and the partner. Both can understand how they have been affected by the incest. Each can find out what the other needs in order to become more emotionally responsive and can persist in moving forward to resolve sexual concerns. When couples work as a team to meet this relationship crisis, they are able to feel closer and more secure with each other. This chapter will focus on what the partner experiences, what each partner needs from the other, and how the couple can work together.

The Partner's Experience

When a survivor has a partner, that partner becomes a victim of incest, too. The intimate relationship is colored by the survivor's early sexual victimization. The partner is powerless to change the past. He or she had nothing to do with the incest and yet must deal with its consequences on a daily basis. Incest becomes an integral part of the partner's life. A partner may easily feel secondary in importance and angry that the survivor has real obstacles to overcome.

Partners are often faced with a dilemma. Energy tends to be focused on the survivor, who needs support in the healing process, yet the partner often has intense feelings that are important to address as well.

Initial reactions to the incest may be shock and disbelief. Anger, frustration, sadness, and helplessness may soon follow. Partners may feel they are unable to assert their own sexual desires and preferences as they struggle to support the survivor. They are likely to have many questions. Some partners are relieved to find out that there is a specific reason for the sexual concerns in their relationship. Some may have difficulty believing the incest really happened, and others may wonder why the survivor didn't stop the incest. Survivors and partners need to allow time for the partner to really understand what happened and to resolve his or her feelings.

The confusion and conflicting feelings one partner was experiencing after five years in a relationship with an incest survivor are expressed here:

Sexuality and love have always gone hand in hand for me. In all my relationships, be they long- or short-term, there has had to be both. I simply cannot separate my heart from my pelvis, nor vice versa.

So when my partner hasn't wanted to be sexual with me, I have often felt a lack of love. This has led to feelings of abandonment, which in turn lead to hurt, resentment, and confusion. The end result has usually been my own withdrawal, emotionally and physically. This makes my partner feel unsafe, so she pulls back also. And round and round it goes.

Being a partner to a survivor has been a very difficult struggle. If there weren't as much love and commitment between us as there is, I doubt that the relationship would have survived.

Incest is ugly. It's painful to look at. It's like an old wound that keeps reinfecting. And it's hard not to take it out on the relationship. I recognize that, out of my own anger and frustration, I have pointed the finger at my partner and blamed her for not relating sexually to me. I have since learned that this only blames the victim and makes her feel worse about herself than she already does. So it behooves neither my partner, myself, nor our relationship.

And yet, I must admit, my frustration is still there. What about my needs, I ask? Why should her needs always take precedence? We were both victims in our childhoods—her of incest, myself of physical abuse. So I didn't have it so easy either. Who's to say whose pain is greater?

My frustration is fueled by feeling that sexuality is so out of my control in this relationship. If I have a partner who is unwilling to be sexual, I have no options whatsoever to share intimacy with her. So I have considered an affair, and we've discussed the idea, but I really don't want one. And I have considered leaving the relationship. But, as I said early on, there exists too much that is loving and good between us for me to leave.

It is common for intimate partners to feel rejected and angry and to be in emotional pain because of the survivor's dislike of sexual contact with them. One man expressed his feelings this way:

I'm lost. I can't figure it out. I'm just hanging in there. I feel like I have to be distant. We're there, but we're not together. I want to talk about it, but I get rebuffed. I don't want to give up. Sometimes I lose my temper and kick toys. Sometimes I wonder what's wrong with me. I feel unattractive and unwanted sexually. Touching her is like touching an electric fence. When we do have sex I feel guilty now 'cause it doesn't feel like making love anymore. It feels worse now after we do it than if we didn't. I don't want to be the bad guy.

And a woman who is in a lesbian relationship shared the following:

When we first met, she was really into sex. I liked her but didn't fall in love with her till after we had been together six months. It seems once I fell in love with her the sex got less and less. We sleep naked in bed together—it seems like there is intimacy—we just don't make love. I don't feel allowed to express my sexual desires because of what it does to her. The few times we have had sex in the past several months, it was either before or after we'd been apart. She always initiates it and wants to have sex only after she's had some alcohol to drink—which I can't stand.

Partners may begin to feel inadequate and wonder whether their way of making love is lacking in some way. Male partners may begin to experience problems getting or maintaining an erection or may doubt their masculinity. Partners of either sex may become overwhelmed with feelings of pain caused by the emotional distance they feel during sex, sometimes without the survivor being aware of it. Resulting sexual problems, such as loss of sexual desire, impotence, and lack of sexual confidence, can become as difficult for the relationship as the sexual problems that originally resulted from the incest.

Partners need to understand that the survivor's dislike of sex stems from the abuse and is not a personal comment on their own sexual attractiveness. From this position they can begin to talk about their desire for mutually agreeable sexual contact within the context of a loving relationship. Intimacy needs are best stated in a nonpressuring manner. For example, a partner might say, "I care for you. I respect you. I want to be physically intimate with you. I do not want you to engage in sex with me unless you really want to. Sex is important to me—it is an expression of my good feelings toward you and of my general satisfaction with being your partner."

Taking an active role in understanding incest helps partners recognize what is happening in their relationship. As one individual explained:

As a partner I must work very, very hard at trying to get some handle on what incest is when I've had no exposure to it. It's very easy to just get angry at the perpetrator and say, "That bastard, I'd like to kill him. I'd just like to blow him away with a sawed-off shotgun." But you can only say that so many times, and that's not doing much in working with the incest and to help build a relationship. You need more than that. So you have to do some research. I think it's important to be involved, and not to be on the outside—like, she's doing the group and the therapy, like that's her problem. I think it's important for partners to really get involved in stretching our minds. We have to stretch our minds to understand how people could be that violent and abusive toward their daughter. It's very hard to work with. Her therapist has done a lot of good work with me so that I can get turned around. I really have to force myself to be able to see the dynamics and how they were played out as she was growing up, because hers is a very severe, violent case.

Since partners also feel victimized by the incest, they may find it hard to manage strong emotional reactions toward members of the survivor's family of origin. Occasionally, partners will feel so angry at the perpetrator or so protective of the survivor that they will move into the role of confronting the perpetrator or the family as a whole. While the desire to do so is understandable, it is not wise to act on it. Such action would take control away from the survivor once again. Whether any confrontation is to occur and how it will happen are decisions the survivor must make. Should she choose to confront her family, support from a partner and a therapist is invaluable.

Feelings also surface toward the nonoffending parent. In the following comment, a partner expresses her feelings about the survivor's mother:

My anger comes with her mother. Her mother is an accessory to the crime, as far as how I perceive it. Her father's a criminal and her mother also committed criminal acts, out of negligence, and there was physical abuse. And the fact that her mother knew when she was six months old that her father was sexually abusing her. And out of fear she chose to sacrifice her daughter—give in to him. That's what it comes down to. So I've had to work a lot in therapy, because we see her mother. We went out and had dinner with her mother last night. It can be so bizarre, because we're sitting there and we're enjoying having dinner together. . . . She's an intelligent woman, she's a marvelous storyteller, loves to laugh. And the three of us are sitting there, and we're having this pleasant conversation, and then it just goes through my head, and my heart, I start feeling those things, and I just want to get up and scream at this person: "Do you know what you did to your daughter by allowing this all those years, when you knew what was going on?!"

Partners of incest survivors may find that the issue of commitment to the relationship takes on major importance. They may hesitate to make long-term plans until they have a sense that the sexual issues can be resolved. The decision to make a commitment cannot be taken lightly, as one partner explained:

It's so easy to fall in love, but it's that daily working at being in love that really matters. It's difficult in the best of situations between two people—it's a lot of work. But when incest is part of that relationship, and it's there all the time, you have to recognize that it exists. I have become a victim of the incest, too. I have to work at how it has victimized me and how it has victimized our relationship. I think that the partner of an incest survivor has to be very serious in deciding not to go into the relationship just to have a superficial relationship and see where it goes. That's never been my tendency to begin with, but I think it's very important when you're dealing with involvement with an incest survivor that you take some time and really say, "Is this something I can handle?" Because I am going to have to give time, energy, and feeling to incest. I'm going to have to be involved if our relationship is going to grow, if we're going to have a partnership. Can I deal with this? This is something serious; this is big. I feel very responsible when I enter a relationship, and I think it's a double edge when it's an incest survivor, because what I'm hearing so often from some of Amy's friends who come over to the house to visit, who are incest survivors, too, the thing I've seen, the common denominator, is, "I'm bad." So if you reject me, it reinforces that I'm a bad, evil person. Because good little girls don't have these things done to them. It would be irresponsible if I were to say, "Oh yeah, well, we'll have this relationship," kind of cavalier. . . . I think it's damaging for anyone to be rejected, but I think for an incest survivor, it is devastating because it reinforces once again the feeling that "I'm no good, nobody could love me, and I've been betrayed." Like Amy will say to me, "I can't believe that you could love me and would want to touch me, that you don't think that I'm unclean, dirty, used." I notice things with Amy, like once in a while she may buy a new article of clothing, but most of the time she goes to used clothing stores. Everything is used. Everything was very black and somber. And very loose fitting, so you really couldn't see any form. I said, "You're not used material!" I came into a little bit of money at the beginning of fall, and I said, "Come on," and we went shopping so she could get some new clothes. I said to her, "You're clean. You're not used. That's not how I perceive you." But that's one of the things that I've had to work out, being with an incest survivor. It's very important for the partner to realize that he or she will become a victim, too, and to deny it or not work with it I think would be the ultimate demise of that relationship. I don't think it can grow. I think eventually it would become so stalemated that you're going to see two people going in two different directions. I could never honestly say that I like incest. It happens to be a factor in our relationship. I mean, if someone said, "You can have a choice of your partner not having a right arm or being an incest survivor," I would rather my partner be without the arm, because it's a hell of a lot easier than to deal with this incest, because it is always there, in hidden ways. It's not going to dissolve overnight. Amy is going to be an incest survivor the rest of her life. We're hoping to grow old together, which means that it's going to be in my life the rest of my life, too. Because it's something that's so different, and you don't deal with, you're not exposed to in any personal way other than in a textbook maybe—and that is so limited, and a lot of that antiquated—that I didn't really know what to do.

What Partners Need from Survivors

Survivors need to develop an understanding of their partner's position, and they need to be responsive to it. They must realize that the partner's life has been touched dramatically by the incest. The partner must play a difficult role at times and it is helpful when the survivor acknowledges this. The survivor can strengthen the relationship by showing appreciation for the partner's support, concern, respect, and patience.

When survivors commit themselves to being in a relationship, it can be very important to recognize that their partner's view of physical intimacy may be substantially different from their own. It can be helpful to really understand the difference. The exchange of caring, sensual touch can give people who were not abused a wonderful feeling of closeness and satisfaction within a partnership. Intimate physical contact between them and their partner may strengthen their love and commitment. Some type of caring touch is an important part of any intimate relationship.

Partners have strong feelings about the incest which must be acknowledged. A survivor can help by really listening to her partner fully. She can help by answering the partner's questions as clearly as possible. A partner who feels truly listened to and heard is likely to find renewed patience for dealing with the incest. The survivor must separate herself enough from the incest to hear how her partner has been affected by it. She does not need to share the feelings her partner has, but she does need to try to understand her partner's experience fully. This will help her develop empathy toward the partner.

Survivors can also help their partners by making themselves available to discuss current concerns about intimacy in the relationship. It is no easy task for a survivor to open herself to hearing her partner's continual disappointment or resentment at the lack of enjoyable physical contact. A survivor has to fight any inclination to interpret her partner's feelings as judgments on her as a person. The feelings can be responded to more positively if they are seen within the context of frustration over what the incest caused.

Ignoring or negatively judging the partner's sexual interest will only create distance in the relationship. While honoring her own limits, the survivor must seriously address her partner's sexual concerns. A partner who has sincerely supported a survivor over a period of time may understandably begin to lose interest if no attempt is made to meet his or her own needs. Initiating touch, sensitively stopping or redirecting touch, and suggesting alternative forms of sexual release that may be comfortable for a survivor are ways she can validate the partner's positive sexuality. A survivor can also support her partner's need and ability to take responsibility for his or her own sexual needs through masturbation. A survivor's communicating her own sexual preferences and needs as well as asking about those of her partner can be very helpful to the partner. This may be difficult for the survivor to do, but it can help avoid unwanted touching and make the touching that does occur as positive an experience as possible for both people.

Sexual expression is one form of intimacy. Alternative forms that a survivor enjoys can be explored and communicated to the partner. Romantic dinners, walks together, long talks, shared baths, foot massages, love letters, unexpected notes, flowers, and small favors are a few ways a survivor can be intimate with her partner without being sexual. Survivors can also express their appreciation to their partners for the support and patience they do receive. And partners often like to hear that they are still seen as sexually attractive and loving.

It is the incest, not the people involved, which deserve the anger.

Partners may need time alone, time with friends, or time with a therapist to deal with their sense of frustration. A survivor can help by encouraging the partner to find healthy ways to express his or her own feelings.

A frequent cause of resentment in partners is the perception that survivors are not really willing to actively overcome the sexual repercussions of the incest. This can feel like more of a rejection than the lack of sex itself. Survivors can provide partners with plenty of current information on how they are doing and can include partners in incest resolution therapy. Survivors need to reassure their partners that they are not denying or running away from intimacy issues. Initiating therapy and touch exercises can help accomplish this. When survivors demonstrate their commitment to resolving sexual issues, partners are encouraged to maintain their commitment to the relationship.

What Survivors Need from Partners

Partners can be most helpful to survivors when they validate the reality of the incest, keep the responsibility for the incest clearly on the perpetrator, and separate the survivor from the abuse she has experienced. When partners learn that their partner was a victim of incest, they may feel upset. They must be careful not to blame the survivor for the incest. Implying or stating that the survivor was responsible or must have asked for the incest can be extremely damaging to her. Such statements only reinforce her irrational feelings of guilt and sense of unworthiness. They may confirm the survivor's worst fears that she will never be believed and loved. It's important that intimate partners understand what the survivor has endured. This can be done by reading about incest, talking with other survivors and their partners, and talking to a therapist.

Becoming knowledgeable about incest enables partners to address concerns in the present relationship in a productive way. Survivors may experience emotional reactions such as crying spells, sleeping problems, nightmares, flashbacks, and painful recollection while resolving incest issues. Understanding that these reactions are normal enables partners to be supportive to survivors. A partner's compassion can alleviate fears, worries, and guilt about the incest. It is helpful for the partner to have at least basic information about what happened to the survivor. The partner can gently encourage the survivor to talk about what happened and how she felt. Calm, nonjudgmental listening is most helpful.

The partner can try to imagine the survivor's position as a child. It may help to recall times in the partner's own childhood when adults were disappointing and hurtful, or times of fear when an older child or adult physically trapped or hurt him or her. From an adult's perspective, the scary childhood event may seem quite minor. Really remembering how one felt as a child, how one depended on adults for survival, and how unequal relationships were in childhood can help. The partner can imagine being the victim of the incest. This exercise can help build empathy when confused feelings exist. Asking questions of the survivor can be beneficial; however, the partner must have the sensitivity to let the survivor share at her own pace. A partner who is overzealous may be seen as pushy, and this approach may remind the survivor of the offender. She might then shut down and reject the partner's well-meaning gestures.

If a partner continues to experience feelings of confusion or blame, he or she can find a counselor who knows about incest and can spend some time working out the feelings so that they don't color the relationship in hidden ways. It is important for the partner to keep talking to the survivor, keep listening, and keep remembering that the incest absolutely was not her fault.

In our study we asked survivors to imagine what a perfect partner would be like. One survivor, who was not currently in a relationship, gave the following response: "I really can't imagine a perfect partner— I'm so turned off to sex. I suppose the person would like nonsexual touch and very little sex. I need emotional support in a big way." Survivors said the most important characteristic for partners was being emotionally responsive and supportive. Table 10–1 shows survivors' responses to the partner characteristics we listed in our questionnaire as well as other traits they listed as desirable. It appears survivors generally want relationships in which sex assumes a low profile and emotional needs take priority.

A partner needs to be an ally to the survivor in making positive changes. So many times partners of survivors either withdraw and emotionally distance themselves from the survivor or pressure the survivor in ways that increase tensions and make problems worse. While resolving sexual problems requires that the survivor and partner work together as a team, partners can increase the relationship's chances of success when they are stable, faithful, and patient. One partner shared the following outlook:

Table 10–1
Partner Characteristics Desired by Incest Survivors

Characteristic	% Desiring Trait
Emotionally responsive and supportive	81
Lets woman know relationship is more important than sex	65
Holds and touches survivor when sex is not the goal	58
Gentle, nonpressuring	35
Supports survivor's freedom to say no to sex	31
Talks about feelings	31
Sensitive	19

Other Traits Survivors Desired:

Lets survivor control speed and
  degree of sexual encounter
Accepting
Loving
Expresses his/her own needs
Fun
Has sense of humor
Trusting
Likes to touch
Respects women
Committed to relationship
High self-esteem
Honest
Strong
Understands incest
Works on own fears
Listens
Believes in God
Responsible

Low sex drive
Romantic
Doesn't always need to be strong
Warm
Outgoing
Rich
Enjoys being sexual
Stable
Healthy
Good parent
Sex is not main issue
Intelligent
Affectionate
Thinks survivor is hot stuff
Sensuous
Is a woman
Comfortable with male and female
  physiology

I think that partners have to be not real ego-oriented when it comes to sexual interplay with the survivor. I think that we have to get our antennae out and be very, very sensitive to that other individual. If we're going to grow and have a healthy, full sexual relationship, we're going to have to be patient and put a lot of sensitivity out there on the line for a long time, to allow this person to be nurtured, and to realize that this is a safe place, this is really safe. And that doesn't come in one, two, three, four times. This is over a period of time. A survivor has to build that trust with her partner.

One survivor responded with appreciation to her partner's involvement:

I feel like I'm real lucky. I feel like I'm really fortunate. I have someone who will work on the incest with me. My partner hasn't known
anything like it, but has really made a commitment to be in there, be
a part of working it out.

Addressing Sexual Concerns Together

Healthy sexual relationships require that both people feel equally
powerful. Survivors and their partners can work together to create
changes that will bring satisfaction to both of them. When adhered to
by each person, the following guidelines can provide a beginning struc-
ture for such cooperation.

Guidelines for Healthy Sexuality

1. Develop general high self-esteem and self-reliance.
2. Discuss sexual concerns openly and honestly and communicate
   feelings without blaming your partner.
3. Acknowledge responsibility for sexual problems.
4. Develop respect and a sense of equality with partner.
5. Assert sexual needs and likes without demanding.
6. Get education and understand the influences of drugs, health,
   stress, and sexual abuse.
7. Establish a variety of comfortable sexual activities in addition to
   intercourse, such as self-stimulation, oral sex, and manual stimulation.
8. Negotiate compromises with respect to your own needs and your
   partner's needs.
9. Approach sexual activity in a relaxed manner, with patience, anti-
   cipating fun and excitement.
10. Accept the natural ebb and flow in sexual desire of yourself and
    your partner.
11. Establish that it's okay to say no at any time.

Lowered sexual desire or withdrawal from sex are concerns couples often experience. Initially, there is a challenge to the intimate partner to be willing to make compromises about his or her need for sex

with the survivor. Partners can facilitate the survivor's sexual recovery by being willing to find acceptable alternatives to whatever forms of sexual activity are upsetting to the survivor. The couple can concentrate on developing mutually pleasurable, nonsexual touch experiences, for example, holding hands or massage. This can be very difficult at first.

A partner who is frustrated by too little sexual contact may become discouraged when asked to expect even less. Partners commonly express the fear that if they stop asking for sex, there will hardly ever be any. This fear, along with the partner's desire for sex, needs to be acknowledged. However, by not being pressured to engage in sexual activity, the survivor can begin to trust that the intimate partner desires to be with her for other reasons besides overt sexual contact. She can then challenge herself to express affection physically, and later sexually, based on her own desire. The eventual result can be a truly willing sexual partner who wants sexual contact rather than a woman who engages in sex because it is expected. Keeping this outcome in mind as a goal can be helpful to partners.

Because of past problems with initiating or engaging in sex, partners and survivors may be awkward and unintentionally insensitive when they make physical contact. The following hypothetical scenario illustrates an instance in which both the survivor and the partner are misunderstood during the initiation of intimate touch.

A male partner approaches a female survivor from behind and touches her breasts in a hugging caress. The survivor responds in a surprised and angry manner and immediately pulls away. The partner feels crushed and rejected. He thinks to himself, "Why doesn't she want me? She's so sexually up tight!" The survivor feels violated and thinks to herself, "That horny beast, if he really loved me he wouldn't be so insensitive!"

In reality, the partner's genuine intention was to be physically affectionate to the survivor—to express his love for her in a close, intimate way. Fearing she might rebuff him if he was more direct, he chose to approach her in an indirect, nonverbal manner. The survivor was caught off guard by his approach, which reminded her of feeling powerless and out of control during the abuse. She interpreted her partner's approach as pressure on her to fulfill his sexual needs. For her, recoiling was a necessary act of self-defense.

This whole unfortunate exchange could have been avoided had the couple communicated their feelings and intentions more clearly. The partner would have been far more successful had he approached the survivor directly in a relaxed manner and said something like, "I want you to know I'm feeling very loving toward you now. I would like to have some physical contact. Sex would be nice, but if you're not into it, I'd like to hug and hold each other. What do you say?" The survivor could have improved the situation had she originally responded with, "I need to be approached verbally, directly, and more slowly. I appreciate your desire to make some contact. Perhaps we can talk and hold each other, or go for a walk. I'm not feeling sexual right now." Thus, by emphasizing a desire for mutually agreeable closeness and contact, partners can compensate for the survivor's tendency to experience them as sexually pressuring. By validating their partners' healthy needs for physical intimacy, survivors can compensate for the partner's tendency to feel personally rejected when the survivor is not interested in sex.

During sexual contact, partners can foster healthy resolution of sexual issues and be sensitive to the survivor's experience by maintaining communication, going slowly, stopping temporarily whenever necessary (such as during a flashback or anxiety attack), and being willing to shift from an intense sexual focus to a loving nonsexual focus if the survivor needs to stop the sexual activity altogether. Experiences such as these, in which the survivor comes to trust the partner's sexual expression, are invaluable in establishing a new orientation toward sexuality.

In the following interchange, the issues of touch and sexual expression were dealt with in a way that built tremendous trust. A survivor, Amy, and her female partner, Sharon, talked about how they learned to resolve problems in creative ways on their own:

SHARON: I'm a toucher. I'm very open. I dive in with my heart before I ever get my mind involved. Amy's very analytical, so we have a very nice balance. But I thought, jeez, how do we do this, you know? When Amy told me she was in love with me, it was a big surprise. It took me a few months to decide, because I'd come out of another relationship, and I really respected Amy and I didn't want it to be a rebound thing. I wanted to know we really wanted to be committed to it, but it was, like, can I touch her? Amy had started to say, about two months before she told me she was in love with me "I need to be touched." Up until that time it was always, "I'm always going to be celibate. I don't want anybody to touch me."

AMY: Yeah, I didn't like people touching me. I still don't like people touching me. I went to the incest group, and we gave upper back massages one time, and I came home and was wiped out the whole night because even though it was someone I knew within my group, I couldn't handle it. I really just couldn't handle it.

SHARON: And that's something I really have to work on. Because to me, before, my reaction would be, What's the big deal? I mean, this is touching, this is great stuff. Well, I'd never had anybody hurt me in a violent way like that. Out of respect for her I didn't let myself get carried away with my own sexual desires. I more or less wanted to do anything in our sexual life where Amy was going to be assertive, Amy would take the initial steps. So she felt that she was in control. She started with her touching me. And that was perfectly fine. She was exploring for the first time, enjoying touching someone else—with no violence and no one else having control, being in a very peaceful, safe place. I became quite aware of that, and that was fine. When I started to touch Amy, I became very aware that she was not feeling. She didn't feel anything for a long time. The first time I gave her a hug, I thought, oh my God—I mean, it was like ramrod straight steel. And I thought, well, you know, if I were in that situation, I would want someone to be really gentle, not bring it into focus a lot, and to be very patient. So that's how we started. And the first time she went to bed, she had nothing on the top, but she had her jeans and her socks on, and the first night we slept together, she slept with her jeans and her socks on. And I used a little bit of humor, and told her it was perfectly all right, and we just took it day by day, and article of clothing by article of clothing, and we finally got down to where even the socks came off. We just did a lot of holding at the beginning.

AMY: Because she's a toucher, one of the things that happened at the beginning of the relationship was that she simply touched me all over without being assertively sexual at all. So what that actually does for me with her is that it makes me very grounded. So that when we moved from just touching, the foreplay is very grounding for me with her. Then we move into heated sexual contact. We did that just naturally, not knowing that that kind of thing would really help me.

Having good, clear communication is the key to resolving many of the problems that arise concerning sex in the relationship. Because the survivor first learned about sex from a sexual offender, she may automatically assume that her partner's thoughts and intentions are similar to those of the offender. She may react anxiously when her partner says such things as "I love you." The survivor may also imagine that the partner is out to satisfy his or her own sexual needs without any real concern for the survivor's emotional welfare.

By talking and working together when negative feelings surface, couples can overcome problems of dissociation, triggers, and flashbacks. In the following exchange a survivor and her partner discussed a technique they developed for resolving a problem they were experiencing with a verbal trigger.

PARTNER: While we would be sexual, particularly in those early stages, I would be very quiet verbally. I wanted to move slowly because she was taking so much in, and not add all the verbal in with it. But I would say to her, "I'm loving you." I would say that over and over again, "I am loving you. This is love." I said it softly and kept saying it over and over, barely whispering it in her ear. She had to relearn the definition of love.

SURVIVOR: During the abuse, my father didn't say, "I'm loving you." He just said, "I love you," or "You love me." It was always in a tone of voice that was very demanding. And when my present partner would first say, "I love you," I would just . . . tighten up.

PARTNER: I noticed her reaction. And that's why I changed it from "I love you" to "I'm loving you," and I kept saying it and saying it. I did it in a whole different way. Well, I thought, just do it very softly—I'm sure he didn't do that. And that's been a change.

SURVIVOR: And now I don't have any problem hearing it. It's one of my favorite things.

Other survivors have stated that degrading terms like "fuck," "cunt," "prick," "bitch," and so on, will automatically remind them of the abuse. Partners may need to refrain from using such language.

Sexual concerns in a relationship can often be lessened through professional therapy. It means a great deal to a survivor when her partner is willing to participate in a treatment program with her. By so doing, the partner reduces the survivor's feeling of being alone and demonstrates his or her own ability to share responsibility for the healing process. The survivor's trust in and respect for her partner increases as she witnesses his or her cooperation in learning new ways of becoming intimate. The partner is relieved to find that the sexual concerns they both share are treatable and that positive change can occur. The relief provided by working together with a therapist was noted by one partner:

> Now that we're seeing a therapist who is trained in this area, we can both recognize the symptoms and patterns of incest as they have manifested in our relationship. At last we know what it is that we're up against, and that is a great help.

Two partners working toward sexual intimacy can make profound changes that will positively strengthen their relationship as a couple. Each appreciates the other's situation, and they learn to balance their needs while still moving forward. Optimism and hope were expressed by this partner:

> Despite all the odds, though, I know we'll beat this thing. We have to, to survive. Rather than letting the incest victimize us both, we need to work towards being teammates together so we can conquer it. We're just starting out.

11
Getting Professional Help

Many survivors and partners of survivors feel anxious about seeking professional help. Picking up the telephone to call a therapist can sometimes be the most difficult step in the entire process. This is understandable, since incest and sexuality are both very personal areas that have long been culturally shrouded in secrecy. Most people are raised with an unspoken rule: Avoid discussing sexual experiences with anybody. Feelings of shame, embarrassment, and fear of what others will think may surface and inhibit people from getting help.

Anxious feelings about therapy can be overcome and replaced with feelings of confidence. By learning what therapy is about as well as how to find a good therapist, survivors and their partners can know what to expect and can help make their experience in therapy a positive one. Because of the betrayal of trust that occurred as a result of the incest, trust is likely to be an issue in therapy. Survivors have learned that they cannot afford to trust blindly; in the past the cost has been too high. They may have difficulty trusting lots of important people in their lives. They can begin by acknowledging that trusting people does not come easily for them. It makes good sense for survivors to maintain an active, informed involvement in all stages of their therapy. Survivors can protect themselves from unproductive or even negative experiences by having guidelines for determining good-quality therapy.

The intent of this chapter is to empower survivors and partners of survivors by offering practical information on different aspects of therapy for incest and sexuality concerns. Counselors and therapists treating incest survivors may also find this chapter helpful for further developing their approaches and skills. The topics covered are (1) understanding therapy, (2) finding a therapist, (3) beginning therapy, (4) incest resolution therapy, and (5) sex therapy.

Understanding Therapy

Therapy is a process whereby a client is able to focus consistent time and energy on resolving problems while utilizing the support and guidance of a trained professional. Most clients attend therapy for a one-hour session once a week, but therapy can take place as often as several times a week or as infrequently as once every several weeks. A session once a week works well for most people as it allows clients to sort out feelings and changes that have occurred during the previous week while still maintaining the momentum necessary to keep working toward their goals. For therapy to work well, clients must be motivated to address their concerns and must be willing to expend energy outside the sessions on activities that complement the therapy sessions themselves; doing individualized exercises, reading books, becoming acquainted with community resources, and reflecting on what came up in therapy the previous week are some examples of such activities.

Counseling sessions usually take place in an informal, relaxed office setting, commonly furnished with living room and office furniture, with a quiet and private atmosphere. Many clients have likened a therapy session to having an undisturbed talk with a concerned friend. While a therapist is certainly concerned with the client's well-being, he or she is not a personal friend in the usual sense. It is the lack of direct involvement in the client's daily life that allows a therapist the objectivity to counsel effectively.

There are several ways to do therapy. They include the following: (1) individual (one client meets alone with one therapist), (2) couple (a couple meets with one therapist), and (3) group or family (approximately three to ten clients meet with one or more therapists). Another method used primarily with couples and families is two therapists working as a team during sessions. This is often a male-female team.

Therapy styles vary from one therapist to another, reflecting both the unique training and personality of the therapist involved. A style used by most is conversational, with the therapist listening to and reflecting back what the client is saying. Some words used to describe the range of differences in style are warm, friendly, supportive, educational, confrontive, or distanced. The same therapist may vary her or his style to complement the personality of a particular client. For instance, a therapist may assertively point out inconsistencies in logic with a highly involved, psychologically strong client; yet with a timid, insecure client, the therapist may maintain a calmer, slower, more nurturing approach. Good therapists have the ability to shift their style in accordance with how their clients are doing on any given day.

Good therapy is neither a comfortable social experience nor an uncomfortable confrontive ordeal. In most cases, therapists will balance a safe, open atmosphere with gentle questioning to maintain progress and will do so at a pace the client can handle. Clients in therapy have a right to question and comment on the process as well as the actual content of the therapy. It is true that some discomfort may occur. Yet for most survivors this discomfort is far less than the discomfort of not going to therapy and continuing to allow the incest to dominate one's life and sexuality.

Survivors and their partners can increase the likelihood of making positive changes in incest-related concerns when they get professional help. Therapists help clients to identify important issues, and they validate the client's feelings. Ongoing therapy provides a consistent time period in which clients can focus their energy completely on resolving identified concerns. Clients learn how to get through periods in the change process that may be uncomfortable or difficult. By offering encouragement, information, and a plan, therapists can counter the tendency, stronger in some than in others, for survivors to give up on themselves. Therapists teach new ways of looking at old problems as well as the necessary skills for changing behaviors, attitudes, and feelings. As one survivor remarked:

> The function of therapy sessions is to keep the stuff coming and to give it direction. Once the client gets some experience with the process, I think the therapist becomes more a facilitator than a director.

Because the repercussions of incest are complex and deep, many survivors and their partners find therapy critical to their healing process. All the women in our study were in individual or group therapy for general incest concerns. Over and over again they emphasized how important they believed therapy had been in helping them to recover. A man who came with his partner to couples therapy regarding sexuality issues shared the following:

> I think a couple in which one person is an incest survivor needs to find a good therapist. A mediator for us has done wonders. We were both too frustrated and pulled apart from each other; we needed a third party to help us see and understand the problem from an experienced point of view.

A twenty-six-year-old survivor who had been married for six years entered therapy when she was pregnant with her fourth child. Her goal was to understand and work out the problems in her sexual life; she was very pessimistic about her chances of success. In her first session, she stated:

> I feel disgusted and disgraced whenever my husband touches me. It feels yicky to me. I resent sex — that it has to be there or else we can't be happy. I wish it didn't exist. Intellectually I know that's not healthy, but that's how I feel. . . . I have good thoughts about him when he's gone.

The progress she and her husband made is evident in the following story, which she wrote three months after therapy began.

> As an adult my memories of when or where the incest started are not real clear. As far as I know I was about three years old. My parents were going through a divorce. My father was the offender. I held him in great esteem. I idolized him and had him on a pedestal. My memories of the incest are of my nipples and genital area being touched. This made me feel very frightened. It was scary not to know why I had to be touched in places that made me feel so different. I didn't like it, so I would cry and cry, but still he never stopped. I would block out what was going on after a certain point. That is what kept my sanity through all the abuse.
>
> The abuse happened various times. Sometimes ten times a year; other times five times a year. It depended on how often I was with my father at his residence. As I grew into a young teenager, I began to view sexuality as something men had to have from women because of their sexual fantasies or desires, which I felt were strong for every boy or man. As I began to use my body sexually, I realized I was enjoying it too. If I became involved with someone who cared for me more than sexually, my body didn't seem to enjoy the sexuality or intimacy. I would run scared and be frightened by any touch from that person.
>
> When I finally did marry, it was to a caring, wonderful husband. He knew about the incest but he didn't really understand it, as I myself didn't at the time. We had a very sexually active life together for about four or five months. At that time he was still enjoying it and I was faking it — afraid of the consequences. I didn't know what they were but I didn't want to disappoint my husband. The honeymoon really seemed to be over. This left me scared. I didn't understand

what was wrong with my body. I was five months pregnant at the time, so I thought maybe that was it. Wrong! I still felt that way between pregnancies. Then I was grasping at straws, never for one minute thinking the incest was the cause. I blamed the fact of child-bearing, nursing, and the stress of all this. But after five years of marriage that had more downs than ups, I felt there must be something physically wrong with my body. A medical doctor advised me that stress and childbearing were the reason. He said that hormones get out of whack and I just needed to give them time to recuperate.

About six months later, I consulted a therapist who told me that incest has a very damaging effect on the mental and physical state of the victims. She explained to me that enjoying sex as a teenager happened because I felt I had something my male counterparts wanted. This was my way of getting attention. In giving my body this way, I could get people to like me. This was a big goal in my life. Once I was married and I began to feel as if I didn't have to do anything to make my husband love me, the sexual desires went away. I realized this guy would love me no matter what. I reverted back to having the feelings I had as a child. I didn't want to touch or be touched.

By this time my husband was very frustrated and ill-tempered a lot. He was understanding things a little, but he didn't change. I was in group therapy for three and a half months. We worked on many issues that helped me feel stronger as a person. I started liking myself and changing in many ways, but my sexuality stayed the same. The group therapy helped me to put the blame for the incest on my father and not myself. I learned simple things about myself, like why it was hard for me to say I'm sorry. I realized I had put my husband into a position of the father image. He in turn would react from the position I had put him in.

When I had gained my new self-image and finished my therapy, my sexual desires came back. They were only temporary, however. Then I was referred to another therapist who specialized in incest and sexual concerns. It seemed as though my sexual life was still deteriorating. My husband and I attended these sessions together. We had more work to do. This time it was our marriage in general and the effects of the last five years that needed work. We learned how to be on each other's side and work together, not against each other. We began to learn about sensate focus and how to touch each other without having to be afraid. By doing this it made me feel very loving and caring about my husband. It gave me a real sense of closeness. He didn't have to feel as though my body was off limits anymore, and I didn't have to worry that his touching me was a sexual thing. We got in touch with how beautiful it is to share our bodies sensually instead of sexually. It brought us back to a beautiful marriage, with lots of ups and fewer downs. By touching each other gently on every point of the body excluding the genitals, we learned how to make and give time to each other. Then we began to touch genitals and realized that was very natural because those were parts of the body too. It drew us closer and closer, and we feel more like two bodies united as one, rather than two bodies afraid of what the other body might do.

I might just say to other survivors to never give up. To finally reach that potential to give love and be loved is a worthwhile commitment that could never be won without proper therapy and the natural human instinct of love. Let the honeymoon begin again!

Finding a Therapist

Professionals who provide therapy for incest survivors fall into several groups, which differ in training specialties, degrees, and fees. Social workers and counselors usually have a master's degree. Psychologists have a doctorate (Ph.D.). Psychiatrists are medical doctors who are able to prescribe medication for mental and emotional problems. It is difficult to generalize about who may be more skilled in dealing with incest and sexuality issues; qualified professionals exist in all categories. The degree is less important than the specialized training a counselor has had. Good backgrounds would include training and experience in incest treatment, sex therapy, couples counseling, family therapy, and depression treatment. A therapist with a background in incest and sex therapy is able to talk comfortably about sexual concerns while sensitively responding to underlying incest concerns. If someone who does both is not available, you may want to ask yourself whether it is more likely that your incest concerns are affecting your sexuality or that your sexual concerns need to be the primary focus of your treatment. This will help you to choose a therapist. One option is to choose a general incest therapist and later pursue more sexually focused treatment with a specialist in sex therapy who has some understanding of incest.

Another consideration in finding a therapist is the sex of the therapist. Many female incest survivors, because of their general apprehension toward males and their fear of possible sexual overtones during the sessions, feel most comfortable with a female therapist. Some male therapists, however, are very effective in working with survivors and provide an opportunity for them to establish a trusting, nonsexual relationship with a nurturing male figure.

Degrees, training, experience, and sex of the therapist are all important issues. Another important issue is the way the survivor and her partner feel about the therapist. Therapists are human beings with their own style, strengths, and weaknesses. While it is not necessary to like the therapist personally in order to have an effective outcome, it is important to trust the therapist. Feeling the respect, caring, and support of a therapist can be a powerful aid to a client in making changes. The personalities of the client and therapist alike will enter into this complex issue. The basic rule is to trust yourself. Pay attention to how comfortable you feel. Comfort is not the only issue to weigh, for therapy is not always comfortable, but strong negative feelings about one particular therapist are enough to eliminate that person from consideration. Other factors, such as the therapist's commitment to the equality of women and men, are not reflected in degrees or titles but can be evaluated through direct questioning or careful listening.

Finding a good therapist can require time and effort. A sensible way to start is to ask for referrals from trusted people and agencies. A family doctor, a gynecologist, a mental health referral service, an incest treatment program, a women's center and resource agency, a rape crisis center, a psychologists' association, a sex therapists' association, and friends can all be asked to supply the names of people they know to have good reputations. Identify the ones who are recommended by more than one source. Call them and ask questions.

When financial constraints exist, look for options. Many mental health clinics and private practitioners have sliding scales to accommodate lower-income clients. Look into insurance coverage on existing medical policies. Some therapists will defer part of the payment until after the therapy has ended in order to spread out payments. If a therapist is appealing but not available, ask her or him to recommend someone else.

While interviewing therapists either on the telephone or in person, you may want to ask the following questions: What is their fee? Is the fee negotiable? Are they willing to have a short initial meeting free of charge? What experience and training do they have in incest and sexuality? What professional memberships do they have—are they licensed, registered, certified? How would they describe their style? What methods do they use? Will they give you the names of physicians or people familiar with their work whom you may call? Take the time to review their answers and think them over. Trust your intuition. Pick the therapist you like best and schedule an appointment.

Sometimes there is a strong client-therapist connection and sometimes there isn't. That is to be expected. However, occasionally a client will begin therapy, then realize she is not working well with the therapist. In such an instance, she may need to stop therapy and change to another therapist with whom she feels more comfortable. However, such a change is most effective when it is clear that the client is making an assertive decision to seek better therapy rather than running away from tough issues. Ideally, this issue would be discussed with the therapist.

A few situations should serve as red flags to leave a therapist. They involve unethical conduct and misinformation. Any therapist who says or implies that the survivor bears any responsibility for the incest is misinformed, and therapy with that person should not be continued. A therapist who suggests or attempts sexual behavior with a client is clearly out of line. This behavior violates every legal and ethical code of professional conduct. Clients should be suspicious of any therapist who even implies that sex with a client could ever be therapeutic. When a client experiences sexual interest from a therapist, the dynamics of incest are recreated. A trusted person in a position of authority again has made sexual advances toward the client when she feels less powerful and psychologically dependent. If this happens, refuse to participate and report it to the professional organization that regulates the therapist. Then find another therapist.

To protect the client and the therapeutic relationship, we recommend that no other type of relationship with the therapist should occur outside of therapy. This includes personal friendship, work exchanges, socializing, and even going out for coffee. When more than one kind of relationship exists, the waters of therapy can too easily be muddied. Even when therapy ends, it is best to keep to this rule. The client may want to return to therapy later, and the therapeutic relationship is altered—compromised—if other relationships have been entered into. Maintaining clear boundaries in the client-therapist relationship provides for the most effective therapy.

Beginning Therapy

The first therapy session can provide an opportunity for both the client and the therapist to get acquainted with one another. The therapist may ascertain from the client the nature of the problem, what previous therapy has been tried, and what the client defines as the goal of treatment. It is also a time to obtain background information on the client and begin assessing the problem in order to formulate a treatment plan. The client can utilize the initial session to find out more about the therapist's background and experiences in treating people with similar concerns and how the therapist might work with her concerns. While the first session is devoted more to establishing rapport and assessing the problem than beginning therapy, a client should leave feeling she or he was heard, having confidence in the therapist's abilities, feeling able to work with the therapist, and feeling hopeful.

Most people enter therapy when they realize they have a problem they have not successfully dealt with alone. The problem may currently be causing them psychological pain or may have a strong potential for causing them future psychological pain. Some people feel excited about entering therapy; others may dread it but feel they can't ignore their problems any longer. A few people enter therapy because they are nearly strong-armed to do so by doctors, partners, or family members who have witnessed the pain they are in on account of unresolved psychological issues.

Incest survivors come to therapy via numerous routes. Most commonly they seek a general therapist rather than a therapist who specializes in treating sexual problems. Many have been experiencing concerns such as eating disorders, problems with sleeping, drug and alcohol dependencies, or problems in interpersonal relationships. Incest is not commonly seen as the root of these concerns. Typically, incest survivors initially exhibit what psychologist Denise Gelinas describes as a disguised presentation.[13] Specifically, the disguised presentation may include symptoms of depression, self-abusive behavior, confusion, impulsive acts, very low self-esteem, and a history of assuming adult responsibilities as a child. Incest survivors tend not to have identified their underlying problem of unresolved incest more directly because (a) as many as 50 percent do not remember the incest, and (b) many who do remember it may consider it irrelevant to their current situation and not even mention it. They may never have defined what happened to them as a form of abuse. Some people were never actually molested but had a parent who behaved seductively toward them. These people can exhibit many of the same concerns as survivors and may be treated by therapists in the same way.

It may take considerable digging on the part of the therapist to discover incest as the source of the symptoms being experienced by the client. A therapist may need to keep pursuing the question over time, as one survivor indicated in the following story:

> I had been in individual counseling for one and a half years. Incest never came up during that time. I was having problems with my social life and relating with other people—and we could never figure out why that was. My therapist had asked me early in therapy if I had been molested. Her question wasn't something I paid any attention to at all—it didn't ring any bells. She asked me again after a year and half of therapy, and my initial reaction again was no, I hadn't been molested. She said she was concerned because a lot of the problems I was having reminded her of the constellation of problems experienced by adults who've been sexually abused as children. The question still troubled me, and that next week I started remembering some stuff with my dad that I had remembered but then thought about in a different way. I said to myself, Maybe that stuff he did wasn't quite right, and began dealing with it in therapy from then on. I had no category for sex as a kid so I never filed it as sexual abuse in my mind.

Many therapists have only recently begun to ask routinely about incest in the early stages of therapy. A therapist will get more information by asking, "Was there any unwanted or confusing touch that happened between family members?" than by asking, "Are you an incest victim?" It is imperative that the incest be identified. Therapy for depression is unlikely to be successful if unresolved incest lies at its root. For this reason, therapists should not be afraid to ask about sexual encounters as a child. When survivors cannot remember their childhood or have very fuzzy memories, incest must always be considered a possibility. People who relate to others with strong feelings of hopelessness, defeat, anger, and overt hostility may also be incest victims.

Some incest survivors first see a therapist who specializes in treating sexual problems. The incest may or may not have been identified.

In these cases the main motivation for therapy may be to address a specific sexual dysfunction, such as lowered arousal, lowered desire, difficulty in achieving orgasm, erection problems or painful intercourse. Other incest survivors enter therapy because they suffer from sexual addiction problems, in which their behavior has become self-abusive or potentially harmful to others. They may be concerned with activities such as compulsive masturbation, compulsive promiscuity, prostitution, sado-masochistic sexual acts, voyeurism, exhibitionism, cross-dressing, and so on. They may have histories of being sexually victimized and of sexually victimizing others. Fear of contracting sexually transmitted diseases that correspond with high frequency indiscriminate sexual activity such as acquired immunodeficiency syndrome (AIDS) may trigger the decision to seek help.

One woman had been in a generally satisfying relationship for over two years and wanted to overcome a chronic feeling of disinterest in sex and an aversion to touching herself and her male partner. She had been sexually molested by her cousins as a child and then made to feel responsible by them for what had happened. Upon entering sex therapy she said, "Sexual issues exist and must be coped with. Ignoring sexuality does not make it go away." As this client demonstrates, motivation for dealing with sexual concerns often stems from a desire to improve the sexual relationship with a partner the survivor cares about.

Sometimes couples enter therapy together to resolve incest issues that affect their current sexual relationship. This can be a very positive approach that affords them an opportunity to address their feelings and concerns and to learn how to communicate about the incest and their sexual relationship without blame or guilt. Couples usually complete therapy with a strengthened bond that comes from jointly tackling a problem that may have once appeared unsolvable.

Therapists who treat sexual problems must be well skilled in assessment. As with general therapists, it is important that they be aware of the possibility that the current sexual problems may relate to previously unidentified, early sexual abuse. When the incest is revealed during the assessment or later in therapy, the therapist must determine the extent to which the sexual problem is a repercussion of the incest. If it is determined that it is indicative of underlying unresolved feelings from the incest, then a treatment plan should be designed to address the incest concerns before or concurrent with the sexual concerns.

On the other hand, the therapist must also be able to assess when the sexual problem is not primarily related to the incest. Some incest survivors believe that all the sexual problems they experience are a result of being "scarred for life" by the incest. But thorough clinical assessment might indicate that the sexual problem reflects a lack of sexual education, a medical problem, or a need for information about sexual techniques. All of these can be easily addressed, and sexual improvement can be achieved relatively soon. For example, a survivor may have never experienced an orgasm during intercourse. Assessment may reveal that lack of adequate stimulation to the clitoris is the main problem.

In the early sessions of sex therapy, most people feel relieved to have found a specialist who is comfortable with the subject of sexuality and who can discuss it in a frank, open, and educational manner. Survivors who have already spent time addressing general incest concerns in individual or group therapy often feel it is a natural progression to then shift to a sexual focus in treatment and address the longstanding sexual problems they have experienced.

Incest Resolution Therapy

Most survivors are ready to address sexuality concerns only after having spent much time working on incest in general. When survivors begin to like themselves and have resolved their feelings about the incest, they may become motivated to reclaim their sexuality for themselves. Thus the initial phases of treatment, here referred to as incest resolution therapy, constitute a time for understanding incest and its impact and for focusing on issues of trust, assertiveness, self-esteem, anger, self-destructiveness, and body image.

The following summary of eight treatment goals developed in 1984 by Faria and Belohlavek illustrates how therapy can create a logical progression toward dealing with sexual content:

1. Establishing involved commitment to the therapeutic process.
2. Identifying old patterns by which the client flees from relationships.
3. Developing a mutual working relationship based on trust and active self-management.
4. Building the client's self-esteem about survival.

5. Developing the constructive expression of anger.

6. Identifying and gaining control over self-destructive and self-defeating behaviors.

7. Networking with other support systems and developing meaningful relationships.

8. Increasing self-esteem through improving body image and understanding human sexual response.[14]

Incest resolution work can take place in either individual or group therapy. Survivors often choose to be in an incest survivors' group after first establishing themselves with an individual therapist. The combination of both individual and group therapy can have a powerful therapeutic effect. Individual therapy establishes a one-on-one relationship with the therapist in which survivors can explore personal issues and concerns in depth.

In group therapy, the therapist spends a limited amount of time focused on each client. However, survivors benefit from watching and hearing other survivors work through their concerns. Group therapy usually has a wonderful way of automatically overcoming the survivor's fear that she is different from others, and the feeling that no other woman or man has the same types of problems. When survivors learn that others have felt and experienced similar things they usually feel enormous relief and hope for themselves.

Because there are other people present, survivors in groups have the choice of taking either an active or passive role in therapy. They can choose to talk about their own issues or to listen to other people. An example of how beneficial a group experience can be was provided by one survivor:

> After doing private counseling, I got to the point where I believed what my body was telling me and could use the words "incest survivor" about myself. I joined an incest survivors' support group that has been an incredible help to me in going through this process— being among a group of women who know, who will listen to your fears, your doubts, your self-hate, and your growing strength. And being there for them, which to me is the same as being able to be there for your own fears, doubts, hate, and strength, is incomparable. *We are not alone.*

Women survivors who are bisexual or lesbian may find it helpful to get into a survivors' group that has other women-oriented survivors. One lesbian survivor commented:

> I know it was very important for me to get into a group with other lesbian incest survivors. The reason I changed groups was because I was in a group without any other lesbians. I never felt any discrimination, but I just didn't feel I could connect on that with anybody else in the group. I felt on the outside, and you tend to feel on the outside anyway. That's another thing, that as an incest victim, when you're going through it, you always feel very separate and different from other people, and that's reinforced, being a lesbian.

Having other lesbians in the group enables lesbian survivors to identify and validate common concerns. For instance, some lesbians may have intense feelings toward the nonoffending mother that may differ from the feelings of heterosexual women. The same lesbian survivor went on to explain:

> There are three lesbians in the group of five women survivors. When any of us talks about our mother, the three of us who are lesbian are a lot more condemning of the nonoffending mother than the two women who are heterosexual. For lesbians, what might make the difference is that the expectations are high for women to be nurturing and loving to women.

Incest resolution therapy encompasses a variety of counseling techniques and approaches for helping survivors to process their feelings. To be useful, a technique needs to feel both comfortable to the therapist and appropriate for the survivor. A partial list of techniques and approaches follows (the order in which they are listed is incidental):

1. *Telling the story.* Telling the therapist (or survivors' group) the details of the incest can provide relief. This can be extremely difficult for some survivors to do. Therapists can encourage each woman to share at a pace that is comfortable for her and to respect her own limits by letting the story come out in parts over the duration of many sessions. Some women do not remember their childhood, and others may visualize scenes from their childhood as in a movie—there are images of events but no feeling memory attached to them. A therapist can help by accepting and encouraging all of these stories.

2. *Reframing.* Events and feelings can be viewed in more than one way, just as a photographer can take a number of different shots of the same subject from different angles. A therapist can help a survivor look at events and behaviors and feelings from a different angle. For example, a survivor may feel that her tendency to "space out" under stress is a negative characteristic that demonstrates her lack of self-worth. She can come to see instead that this was a very positive way in which she coped with the overwhelming stress of incest. It is evidence of her strength and creativity in coping with a traumatic event. She may find that she wants to feel more conscious control in choosing this coping strategy, or she may decide that spacing out is no longer helpful to her as an adult and that she is ready to learn new coping skills. She can then begin to find more appropriate ways to cope.

3. *Power and responsibility.* Many survivors can benefit from a close look at their power and their responsibility. First, a survivor must understand that she absolutely was not at fault and was not responsible for the incest. Believing this can eliminate tremendous guilt. Next, a woman can learn to see how she may have taken on the passive role of a victim and carried that into her adult life. She can learn to appreciate her own power now and begin to take responsibility for changing the parts of her life she does not like. A therapist must be careful to help her learn how to balance this process and how to view the ability to change in a realistic time frame. For another survivor who reacted to her victimization by becoming aggressive and domineering, the therapeutic challenge may involve helping her learn to recognize and respect the rights of others.

4. *Communication skills.* Survivors found as children that their needs and wants were not respected, and often they did not learn effective communication skills. Assertiveness training, owning one's feelings and desires, active listening, and so on, can be very helpful in reclaiming personal power.

5. *Review of personal and sexual history.* Patterns of behavior can be gleaned from a review of the survivor's life. Awareness of these patterns and how they develop can help the survivor make choices about which patterns she wants to change.

6. *Finding the child.* All adults have a child within. For the survivor, discovering and nurturing the lost child within her can be a major

part of therapy. Hearing what the child wants and feels is the first step toward meeting her needs. Survivors are frequently great at giving to everyone but themselves. Learning to balance the adult and the child, to integrate both within herself, is a big task. It can be helpful to look at particular situations that indicate whether a survivor is initiating and responding from her child part or from her adult part. She can then choose which is most comfortable for her in a given situation. For example, the child part of a woman is not the best part to have uppermost when balancing a checkbook but is definitely the best to call forth for playful, relaxed sexual activity. The principles of transactional analysis (TA) may be useful here.

7. *Gestalt.* Gestalt techniques, particularly chair work, can be very powerful. Chair work involves the survivor imagining that someone she has things to say to is sitting in an empty chair in the room. She can talk to the person, taking time to stop and get her thoughts clear and explore her feelings in a way she could not easily do if the person were actually in the room. In this way, a survivor can express sadness and anger to the offender, parent, and others who played a role in her past. This can be particularly effective when someone has died, is geographically distant, or is inappropriate to confront, or in preparation for an actual discussion or confrontation.

8. *Visualizations and affirmations.* A survivor can learn to visualize, that is, see pictures in her mind of herself acting and being the specific way she would like to be. She can also use an affirmation or statement, such as "I am a beautiful, strong woman right now," and repeat it out loud and/or write it over and over to help herself begin to believe it.

9. *Rational emotive therapy.* A survivor can discover how her thoughts affect her feelings and influence her actions. She can learn to change unproductive thoughts. Challenging irrational, limiting beliefs about how things should be can produce new thought patterns and new behavior.

10. *Relaxation and hypnosis.* Relaxation techniques to help a woman ground herself and release tension are very useful tools. Hypnosis can help a woman reconnect with times and experiences in which she felt strong and competent. Hypnosis can be used to gain access to old memories, previously out of conscious reach. Therapists

must take care not to go too far too fast and to avoid overwhelming the survivor with too many memories or with memories of an intense nature. Therapists should have a clear purpose in mind for bringing back the memories.

11. *Journals.* Keeping a written record of feelings, thoughts, experiences, and insights between sessions can be a very useful experience for a survivor. In addition to the benefits of acknowledging feelings and thoughts, a journal is a useful transition tool which a survivor can continue to use after therapy is over. It is not necessary for the therapist to read the journal. It can be useful to the survivor to feel she has sole control over the content and that she can share parts of it with the therapist if she chooses to do so.

12. *Dreams.* Dreams provide messages from the unconscious and can help a survivor understand herself and her feelings better. Helping the survivor learn to interpret her own dreams enhances her power and self-confidence.

13. *Psychodrama.* Acting out a situation from the past or one she anticipates in the future can provide a survivor with an immediate experience of her feelings and an opportunity to experiment with new responses. Psychodrama can also help the survivor see situations from other people's perspectives. Psychodrama can be an intense experience for the survivor and thus requires the therapist be well-trained in doing it.

14. *Body work.* Bioenergetics, Hakomi, and other physical therapies offer helpful techniques. They can provide opportunities for emotional understanding and release. Grounding and breathing exercises increase a survivor's sense of control and personal power. However, therapists must be careful not to touch a survivor more than she is comfortable with and not to overwhelm her with physical exercises that might result in her feeling out of control.

15. *Letter writing.* Letters to others, living or dead, can help a survivor direct hurt and angry feelings outward instead of holding them inside. Often letters are never sent; the benefit is in writing them. For some survivors, actually sending the letter or confronting someone directly with a letter may be appropriate. A therapist can help weigh potential benefits and problems.

16. *Family therapy.* Family members can join the survivor in sessions with the therapist. They can be members of the original family (where the incest occurred) or members of the survivor's subse-

quent family, that is, spouse and children. Therapists who choose to work with the original family should be specifically trained in family systems theory and especially proficient in treating dysfunctional family systems. Survivors may want to utilize a safe, supportive therapeutic setting for disclosing the incest and its effects to the original family. Family therapy offers a possibility for survivors to directly break from a victim role in the family, to obtain a broader perspective on what other family members experienced, and perhaps to reconnect with old family members in new, healthier ways. However, there is a risk involved—family therapy may bring about negative confrontations and thus may not result in family closeness. A therapist can help the survivor weigh the possible outcomes of this approach.

To be effective with any technique, the therapist must first build strong rapport with the survivor. The survivor needs to feel that the therapist is present, listening fully to her, and trustworthy. Confidentiality is extremely important.

Another important issue in incest resolution is loyalty. The therapist must walk a fine line in order to keep full responsibility for the incest on the offender without attacking him. Bonds between parents and children are strong, and many survivors feel loving and loyal feelings toward the offender. A therapist must paint the picture of the offender as a person with positive qualities who lacked impulse control and made destructive choices; otherwise, the survivor may easily feel compelled to defend him to the therapist. If the survivor feels that the therapist will not see the offender as a monster, she will feel safer to explore all her feelings toward him.

The cornerstone of all techniques and approaches in incest resolution is an emphasis on the survivor learning how to find and use her own power. While maintaining a supportive, nurturing relationship to the survivor, the therapist must be able to encourage the survivor's own expression of assertive strength and action. Healthy therapist-survivor relationships are indicated when (1) survivors feel free to take the lead in suggesting problem areas that they want to address, (2) survivors feel comfortable to express feelings such as confusion, anger, and appreciation to the therapist, and (3) survivors feel that their own opinions, judgments, and ideas are as worthy of expression and discussion as those of the therapist.

Therapists can help survivors to recognize the importance of the survival skills that were developed in response to the sexual abuse. Often survivors are very talented and capable in many areas of their lives, socially and professionally, despite the abuse. Self-esteem can be enhanced when survivors are able to give themselves credit for the positive personality traits that they developed in response to the confusing sexual experiences of childhood. They can learn to feel proud of their ability to survive and still grow as individuals despite having been raised in a chaotic lifestyle.

Because of the special type of abuse experienced by survivors in their formative years, therapists must relate to survivors with sensitivity, care, and respect. Physical contact in terms of hugs or pats may be inappropriate until such time as the survivor feels comfortable and gives permission for the touch. Touch may trigger feelings of helplessness and confusion, with the survivor again perceiving herself to be less powerful. When touching occurs, it should be clearly nonsexual and should always respect the survivor's best interests—not the therapist's need for reassurance or contact.

Incest resolution therapy is usually long-term, often lasting from one to several years. The amount of time required for therapy depends on the individual and her needs. Some survivors choose to take breaks from therapy and then come back to it over the course of many years. Others may choose shorter-term therapy and then work on the issues away from therapy. Resolving the issues of trust, self-esteem, assertiveness, anger, and so on, can have profound effects on a survivor's life and can open her to the option of reclaiming her sexuality.

Sex Therapy

As survivors begin to experience a sense of resolution regarding general incest issues, and as they develop skills in liking, respecting, and taking care of their own bodies, they may naturally progress toward wanting to address sexuality concerns. Faria and Belohlavek explain:

> Because the body has been used and abused, time must be spent on integrating it as a part of the total person. Aiding the client in knowing her body through exercise, diet, and self-pleasure is the beginning of the process in which she assumes responsibility for and gains control of her body. Education in sexuality and physiological response can assist her in relieving the guilt she may have because of past

responses to sexual stimulation from the violator. As the woman accepts control over her body, issues such as sexual dysfunction, sexual preference, intimacy and love can then become a therapeutic focus.[15]

Feeling good about oneself sexually is in itself therapeutic. Benefits include a more pleasant sexual relationship, increased self-confidence, self-awareness, and comfort. Every person is sexual. The positive recognition of her sexuality can help a survivor feel more relaxed in all aspects of her life.

To be motivated to focus on sexuality concerns, survivors need to (a) recognize the unfairness of their situation, (b) believe they are entitled to something more, and (c) make a decision to *reclaim* the sexual part of themselves. Incest resolution therapy can succeed in helping survivors get to this point and can establish a basis for any sex therapy to come. As one survivor suggested to therapists:

> Encourage survivors to tell what happened, help them see how their problems today stem from the incest, help them understand who was responsible, let them express their emotions about it, encourage them that there is nothing wrong with them—the sexual problems are a symptom of the abuse.

Teen survivors receiving group therapy for the incest may be very eager to gain some resolution concerning sexual issues. Embarrassment, fear, and previous lack of permission to discuss sexuality may hold them back. To compensate for this, adult group leaders, teen group members, and parents may want to jointly plan a series of group meetings specifically focusing on sex. Guest speakers, films, and written materials could be used. Ideas for topics include the following:

1. *Sex education.* Gaining accurate information regarding sexual functioning, drives, behaviors, feelings, and so on.
2. *Self-defense.* Developing skills in verbal and physical self-protection; distinguishing between exploitive and caring touch; learning how to determine a person's potential for sexual abuse.
3. *Relationships.* Learning about sex roles, normal dating sequences, how to choose a partner, positive partner traits, assertiveness, and how sex fits into a relationship.

Early intervention regarding sexual concerns can spare teen survivors years of unhappiness and insecurity. Adult survivors' groups may wish to integrate similar topics into their formats. It can be helpful for adult survivors to share among themselves how they feel incest may have affected their sexuality and what they have done to help themselves overcome their sexual concerns.

Sex therapy is a special type of therapy used to treat specific identifiable sexual concerns such as difficulty in achieving orgasm, pain with intercourse, erectile or ejaculatory problems, inhibited sexual desire, and discrepancies of sexual interest in couples. It tends to follow a brief therapy format in which therapy lasts for only two to six months and in which behavior change is the goal.

Only a small percentage of therapists specialize in sex therapy. Many receive training in sex therapy as part of professional licensure requirements or because of an individual interest in the specialty. The national organization that certifies sex therapists is the American Association of Sex Educators, Counselors, and Therapists (AASECT). Sex therapists must be able to assess sexual problems with regard to medical, relationship, and psychological influences. In many cases, they work closely with medical doctors such as gynecologists, urologists, and family practitioners in assessing and treating the sexual problem.

Survivors find that sex therapy sessions are very similar to general counseling sessions. The only noticeable difference is that sexuality is discussed quite openly and in more detail. Progressive exercises, which are to be done by the client (alone or with a partner) at home between the sessions, are usually given as homework. Sex-focused therapy thus demands a commitment of time and energy to learning outside the therapy sessions through regularly practiced, structured exercises. This structured learning is an essential part of treatment and is effective in undoing the old behaviors and patterns of sexual responding that had developed as a result of the incest. When clients are motivated and persistent in their at-home exercises, the treatment techniques have very high success rates.

Sex therapy techniques that are used routinely with adult survivors include the following:

1. *Sex education (in session).* The client learns about female and male sex drives, human sexual response cycles, and anatomical

functioning. Myths and misconceptions about sex are dispelled, and new information is provided.

2. *Self-awareness (at-home exercise).* After verbal instruction in the therapy session, the client spends time at home acquainting herself with the look and feel of her own body. Over the course of several weeks, she may view herself in a mirror (identifying body image concerns), massage herself (identifying self-pleasuring concerns), and become familiar with the look and feel of sexual areas (naming parts, learning techniques to enhance arousal and orgasm). Male clients learn and practice self-awareness exercises to improve pleasuring, stimulation, and control techniques.

3. *Desensitization (in session, at home).* The client learns relaxation skills and/or hypnosis. She later practices these skills to feel comfortable visualizing images of progressively more overt sexual material. Problems such as painful intercourse and vaginal tightness are often treated with a desensitization technique done at home using graduated sizes of vaginal dilators. Vaginal dilators are medical devices shaped like test tubes. They are made of a hygienic plastic and vary in size from four inches long and the diameter of a thin pencil to six inches long and about an inch and a quarter in diameter. They come in about six graduated sizes. The client learns mental and physical techniques to facilitate insertion of dilators for prolonged periods of time (up to twenty minutes a day), starting with the smallest size. Desensitization techniques work well to overcome fears. The client remains relaxed and in control while moving forward therapeutically.

4. *Aversive conditioning (in session, and as needed at home).* This technique is occasionally used to help the client overcome strong undesired associations, such as sexual attraction to violence. The client imagines the sexual stimuli (that is, fantasies of violent sexual activities) and then introduces aversive stimuli such as ammonia held under the nose, moderate electric shock, or mental pictures of repulsive behavior like vomiting. Repeating this sequence creates a new association (for example, sexual violence and ammonia) and therefore breaks the old association. As arousal from and sexual response to the negative images are reduced, the client is freed to develop new patterns for sexual stimulation.

5. *Communication (in session).* Partners learn techniques for discussing sexual likes, dislikes, and concerns in a productive, non-

threatening manner. An important goal of therapy is the comfortable communication of specific sexual techniques so that changes can be made.

6. *Sensate focus (a series of progressive, at-home exercises done with a partner).* The purpose of sensate focus is to learn to relate in a physically intimate way without feeling pressure for sexual interaction, and to integrate communication skills previously learned. The partners take turns exchanging touch in a safe setting (there is a temporary ban on overt sexual activity). Changes are made slowly, and the tone is nondemanding. Eventually, over the course of weeks, the touching progresses into more overt and direct sexual activity. Sensate exercises are defined in three phases. Sensate phase one maintains the focus on the giver of the touch as she or he learns how it feels to explore and touch the receiver's body for her or his own pleasure. Breasts and genitals and intercourse are initially off limits. The receiver is quiet unless the touch is unpleasant. Sensate phase two involves the receiver giving verbal and gentle physical demonstrations to the giver on how she or he likes to be touched. Sensate phase three concentrates on teaching and learning stimulation techniques for the sexually sensitive parts of the body.

Sensate focus is probably the most important sex therapy technique available to a survivor and her partner, and the results of treatment are impressive. McGuire and Wagner found in 1978 that survivors responded well to an extended period of sensate focus exercises. They identified three important treatment issues that are addressed in detail.

The first issue involves the *identification and expression of the patient's repressed anger.* As the sensate focus progresses, the patient may experience tremendous rage but may not easily become aware that she had associated the molesting adult of her childhood with her current partner. The angry feelings at the sense of violation as a child were rarely if ever expressed directly at the parent or parent-surrogate, but rather they were later acted out in relationships with other men through teasing, nonresponsiveness, or outright avoidance of sexual contact. She must be helped to differentiate these male figures by encouraging verbalizations of direct anger about her early experiences and explaining the mechanism of displacement.

The second treatment focus is that of *control of the initiation and pacing of the sensate focus exercises.* It is important that the patient be given control to initiate sexual or sensual contact and to limit or extend the type of contact. This is a technical deviation from the typical sensate focus in which both partners alternate initiation of the sessions. This helps to counteract the sense of helplessness in the face of sexual approach engendered in the childhood and internalizes the locus of control. Many women need to maintain control in the initiation and in the extent of contact after treatment.

As the sensate focus progresses, the therapist must be sensitive to expressions of *guilt associated with the experience of sexual pleasure.* Childhood stimulation is pleasurable in varying degrees, yet clearly forbidden. The child learns to associate feelings of sexual attention and pleasure with guilt and, later, to repress feelings of pleasure. The permission giving and support from the therapist are exceedingly important in the resolution of feelings of guilt.[16]

Typically, sex therapy for survivors moves more slowly than with nonsurvivor clients, since survivors may be easily overwhelmed by sexual activity and may require plenty of time to assimilate what they are experiencing. The importance of this slow progress is demonstrated by an incident that occurred during couples therapy. Due to a broken light bulb in a projector, the therapist was unable to show a short film that depicted a couple doing the sensate focus exercise. Instead she verbally described the techniques and gave a written handout to the clients. The couple proceeded to do the exercises at home several times a week for three weeks. They were excited about their progress. After the third week, it was time to begin allowing touch of genitals and breasts. The couple came in and reported on how things went. The survivor stated it was difficult to feel her partner's penis because his zipper was in the way. The therapist was shocked to find out that the couple had been doing the exercises with their clothes on all that time. It was a profound, indirect communication from the survivor of her need to pace exercises and to begin with nonthreatening contact. The next week the couple progressed with ease to doing the exercises with no clothes. The survivor said she was glad she had experienced the clothes-on sessions to start. Since then, when appropriate, the therapist has incorporated clothes-on instructions in working with survivors.

The following treatment progression is a sample of what can happen in couples' sex therapy on a week-by-week basis. This sample describes a treatment plan for a survivor and her partner who wanted to resolve problems of inhibited sexual desire, anxiety about touch, and fear of sex. Other couples might move more slowly or more quickly through the plan. Any treatment plan should be flexible and should be individualized for the people involved.

Weekly Plan for Sex Therapy with Couples When There Is a History of Incest

SESSION 1 Intake and assessment
- Explore history in detail; this may require more than one session.
- Determine level of relationship strength and commitment.
- Outline sexual and general relationship ups and downs.
- Assess current stresses on relationship.
- Get specific description of sexual problems.
- Assess for possible medical factors.
- Describe treatment process.
- Develop treatment plan.
- Have individual sessions for information gathering and expression of personal frustrations, beliefs, and perceptions.
- Establish ground rule that couple can engage in sex only when survivor really wants to and initiates it. Deal with possible fears of partner that this may mean no sex for a given period of time.

SESSION 2 Explore what sex means to each partner by asking them to share their mental associations with the word "sex" and sexual activity.
- Go over "Guidelines for Healthy Sexuality" in chapter 10 and CERTS conditions in chapter 1 (does current sexual relationship meet these criteria?), concept of taking responsibility for own sexual needs, that is, not making partner responsible for one's own sexual fulfillment.

- Introduce concept of sex as shared fun activity.
- Discuss creating a situation in which there's no pressure to perform or engage in sex; discuss sex as a choice, not a duty.

SESSION 3 Influences of incest

- Discuss incest in general, along with the specific experiences of the survivor. Emphasis is on raising partner's awareness of what survivor endured and how it affected her or him.
- Discuss importance of nonsexual touch and nurturance.
- Discuss similarities and differences between partner and offender.
- Identify issues from partner's past that may be affecting current situation, for example, fear of abandonment, rejection, perceived sexual inadequacy.

SESSION 4 Relationship issues

- Introduce concept of working as equals in a team.
- Help couple avoid allowing themselves to become enemies to each other. Make the sexual repercussions of incest the enemy. Focus on inventing creative solutions together.
- Process current anger and resentments.
- Emphasize caring and contact.
- Deemphasize sex and encourage other forms of touch.
- Reframe sex as one of many forms for expressing positive feelings.
- Give assignment (three home sessions): hand holding, hand-foot massage, hugging, sitting close.

SESSION 5 List messages about sex from the offender. Explore offender's distorted thinking about sex.

- Find out about specific sexual experiences with offender, how survivor felt at the time physically and emotionally, and survivor's beliefs about what was happening and why.

- Have partner share how his/her thinking about sex differs from that of the offender.
- Explore body-image issues of survivor.
- Give assignment (three home sessions): Sensate Focus I—touch with clothes on, no genital or breast touching, emphasis on touch for the benefit and exploration of the giver; survivor goes first as giver.

SESSION 6 Concept of conditioning

- Introduce concept of conditioning and explain how to deal with challenges to undo it; associate new feelings with feelings of sexual arousal and pleasure.
- Introduce concept of dissociating.
- Reframe problem of dissociation as positive and important form of self-protection at the time of the incest.
- Discuss concept of triggers and flashbacks specific to survivor; focus on developing ways survivor and partner can work together to address these.
- Give assignment (three home sessions): Sensate Focus I—with touching of genital and breast areas included, clothes on.

SESSION 7 Discussion and reflection on male-female sex roles, family influences, role survivor played in original family.

- Look at current relationship dynamics.
- Discuss importance of equality in sexual contact, possibilities for stepping out of roles.
- Develop skills for each person to initiate or stop sexual contact.
- Give assignment (three home sessions): Sensate Focus I—with clothes off; two sessions with no touching of breasts or genitals; one session with touching of breasts and genitals included.

SESSION 8 Discussion of sensate focus exercises.

- Assess current concerns and accomplishments in making changes.

- Give assignment (three home sessions): Sensate Focus II—with clothes off.

SESSION 9 Ending treatment

THROUGH
LAST
SESSION

- Discuss approaches to sexual contact, how to initiate sexual contact.
- Discuss importance of being direct and having clear communication.
- Deal with concerns brought out by Sensate Focus exercises, relationship dynamics.
- Explore concepts of sexual harmony and satisfaction.
- Discuss what couple will do to deal with problems that might resurface and need more work; point out that this is not unusual.
- Discuss and brainstorm to address hypothetical problems that could cause relapse.
- Give home assignment: Sensate Focus III—modify to specific needs of survivor; begin with her as receiver. Eventually focus on resolution of other sexual problems, such as difficulty in achieving orgasm. Begin to reduce frequency of sessions, then have follow-up visits only.

Treatment for sexual problems combines general counseling techniques, as described in the previous section on incest resolution therapy, with specific behavior-change techniques for treating sexual dysfunctions. Therapists need to be flexible in using and altering techniques so as to be sensitive to the needs of each individual client. When therapists exercise creativity in tailor-making interventions for incest survivors, they can generate an unlimited number of effective techniques. Many techniques can be adapted to address sexual concerns.

One incest resolution technique consists of finding the child within oneself and learning to listen to her and nurture her. This can be sexually focused by encouraging the survivor to discover and nurture her sexual innocence, playfulness, and ability to seek pleasure for pleasure's sake. This involves reeducating the body about physical innocence and safety.

By inventing their own personal cleansing ritual, survivors can reclaim their bodies for themselves. Similar to a baptismal ceremony, body cleansing can be coupled with a series of positive affirmations concerning each part of the body. Thus a survivor might hold up her arm as she soaps it and say, "Now I am reclaiming my arm for myself and my own pleasure. Every cell in my arm is now giving up its association with touch from the offender. I am in control. I have nothing to be afraid of anymore. I reclaim the innocence of this part of my body. I belong to me. I reclaim my body and my sensation for me. I reestablish the innocence of the skin, hair, and nerves of my arm. I go back to the innocence my skin had as a baby. My arm is mine, strong and pure."

Gestalt techniques work well in sex therapy for giving survivors insight into and the ability to assert their developing positive sexuality. In a technique developed to help treat inhibited sexual desire, the survivor tells the offender (imagined to be sitting in a chair) how his way of relating sexually was distorted and abusive. From that exercise the survivor can get in touch with her conditions for positive sexual relating. And in treating a couple in which the survivor is afraid of sex, a combined exercise of gestalt and psychodrama can work well to help the partner understand and empathize with the survivor's inner experience. The survivor stands behind her partner, who has assumed the role of the survivor, with her hands gently resting on her partner's shoulder. She then shares out loud her inner thought processes and physiological sensations as she imagines step-by-step her partner's sexual approach. The exercise can be built upon to allow the survivor and her partner to create alternative means of sexual approach that would be more comfortably received.

Triggers can be treated by developing techniques that encourage the breaking of old associations and the establishing of new and positive ones. For example, a survivor who becomes upset by looking at or touching male chest hair can embark on a series of exercises in which she looks at and relates to her partner's chest hair in a totally new manner. She might, for example, repeatedly shampoo it and draw pictures in it with her fingers. Ongoing relaxation and massage techniques can be incorporated to gradually desensitize her to the old impact of the chest hair. Even a trigger such as heavy breathing can be addressed in therapy by having the survivor develop new associations with the sound. For instance, the survivor and her partner can repeatedly practice heavy breathing together during a nonsexual time. The survivor always breathes a little louder than her partner, increasing the loudness when possible. A song chosen by the survivor can be taped and played while the survivor practices heavy breathing to it.

Feeling upset with viewing and touching her partner's penis is a common issue for a survivor who was forced to masturbate the offender's penis, or who was sodomized or raped. Penis fear can be addressed using techniques that encourage control and a relaxed opportunity to begin thinking of her partner's penis in a new light. Partners must be willing to engage in these exercises passively and without giving any suggestion that they want stimulation or orgasm to occur. One survivor and her partner worked out an exercise in which she covered her partner's penis with her favorite chocolate mousse and then touched the penis with her fingers and licked it off. Another survivor practiced sitting far from her husband as he sat with an erection (she began with sitting in the next room!), and then moved progressively closer. Seemingly silly techniques can be very effective, for instance, drawing a face on a partner's penis and then talking to the penis as if it were a puppet.

The key in creating techniques for triggers is to have the survivor gain control by actively, assertively, and creatively changing old associations to new ones. Incorporating humor can be wonderfully effective, as it encourages the survivor to experience sex as a relaxed, fun activity.

To be good at treating the sexual problems of survivors, therapists must be able to recognize survivors' special needs and alter established approaches accordingly. For survivors, sex is usually highly charged. As they let go of old methods of self-protection and focus on experiencing pleasure in sex, they invariably will feel vulnerable and emotional. Therapists have to find a balance between encouraging the survivor to open to sex more fully and respecting the survivor's need to withdraw and protect herself. New stresses can produce temporary setbacks that bring with them old feelings of hopelessness. This is the time to get back on track and have faith in the recovery process. Accepting the up-and-down nature of sexual recovery is important so that survivors, their partners, and therapists can continue to focus on sexual concerns with persistence and optimism.

12
The Survivor's Choice

Incest survivors are victims of trauma. A profoundly negative experience occurred in their lives—an experience over which they had no control and no escape. Nothing can erase the pain from the past; memories do not dissolve. However, incest survivors do have a choice. They can let the pain from the past continue to control and victimize them or they can make a conscious choice to leave the victim role behind. It's not easy. It's not possible to leave the victim's experience behind by willing it to be that way. It takes facing the incest and its repercussions head on. It takes hard work and a long time. It can be the most worthwhile and important choice a survivor will make in her entire life. A survivor's discovery of herself can be a magnificent experience full of wonderful surprises. As one survivor advised, "Remember that other women share the same feelings as you and that they do get better. The experience of incest won't go away, but you can reveal to yourself many hidden strengths."

Overcoming the effects of past abuse can be a very rewarding, empowering experience. Initially, it can be scary to turn and face past abuse directly, with one's eyes open. It can be hard to realize how families let people down and even exploited them. Admitting the need for and seeking outside help may be a difficult step. But frequently, in time, survivors find tremendous relief in knowing they are not alone and that there are effective ways out of their current psychological and sexual dilemmas. Survivors learn to validate their self-protection and survival skills. They come to acknowledge their lost innocence and begin responding in assertive, nurturing ways in order to meet their own needs. Such feelings as guilt, anger, and sadness can be expressed and resolved, permitting survivors to deepen intimacy and trust in relationships with other people. By understanding what happened, why it happened, and how it happened, survivors can emerge from confusion and fear, able to face new experiences with confidence.

Survivors are often surprised at how well they are able to over-come the sexual repercussions of incest once they have committed the time and energy it takes to effectively address these issues. One partner of a survivor expressed delight in the success they had been experiencing sexually after working patiently on sexual inhibition for a year.

> Early in the relationship I became aware that Fran did not feel anything when I touched her. It has been wonderful watching different parts of Fran's body literally coming alive. When I think back when she was like a steel rod, I remember asking her if she would mind if I would kiss her and she would look at me and say, "What? You mean on the mouth?" Fran thought she might throw up if I kissed her. Now I contrast that with three days ago when Fran turned to me and joked, "Well, when are we going to make love?" In a year's time, this is phenomenal!

Survivors can reclaim their sexuality *for themselves.* They can experience feeling comfortable with their bodies and with giving and receiving physical pleasure. Touching can become a positive, nurturing experience. Survivors can gain more control over their bodies and can experience sexual fulfillment. Sexual problems and inhibitions can be overcome in ways that strengthen survivors' feelings of personal respect and self-esteem. Healing the sexual trauma of incest can have a positive effect on the survivor's current family. A survivor shared in therapy her happiness at discovering that her eldest daughter was warming up to her husband's friendly affection for her. The daughter had been mimicking the mother's old behavior, recoiling from the touches of an adult male. As the mother worked through her sexual inhibitions and enjoyed snuggling with her husband on the couch in the evenings, all the children became more open and relaxed about physical displays of affection.

Sexual healing is a beautiful gift a survivor can give herself. The sexual repercussions of the incest can be understood, challenged, and worked through. When a survivor makes the choice to face the incest directly, her burden of pain and hurt can be lifted. The incest will always be part of her past, but she can choose to remove its hold on her life. A survivor *can* claim her identity as a healthy, sexual person. The choice is hers.

Appendix A
Sexuality Concerns of Male
Incest Survivors

This appendix has been written especially for male incest survivors and for other readers interested in how childhood incest experiences may affect male sexuality. By gaining knowledge and awareness, male survivors, like their female counterparts, can learn that they are not alone, that they are not unique in their sexual concerns, and that there are ways out of their present sexual and emotional dilemmas.

Theory and conclusions presented in this appendix have been derived from clinical experience, general readings, self-reports of male survivors, and consultation with professionals who specialize in treating male survivors. Sadly, existing research on the relationship between incest and male sexuality is scant.

Both male and female survivors share many similar sexual concerns as a result of incest. As with female survivors, the incest itself has a major effect on the male's psychological and social development in childhood. The incestuous activity represents an extreme betrayal of trust and abuse of power between the victim and the offending family member; it violates important physical and emotional boundaries and reduces or destroys the victim's sense of privacy. Young males who are seduced or coerced into premature sexual activity are denied the opportunity to be genuinely consenting partners. Consequently, the sexual abuse often creates feelings of low self-esteem, fear, confusion, guilt, and humiliation—feelings that may hinder many aspects of social and psychological development. Having to maintain the secret of the abuse and living with the fear of further abuse can create continual feelings of stress and conflict, thus taking a tremendous toll on a boy.

Because he might have had pleasurable physical sensations during the abuse, a boy may experience conflict about the experience. A part of him may yearn for repetition of the sexual contact. When this occurs, further confusion and guilt are added to his emotional load. He may feel tremendous self-loathing. He may manifest the stress by having difficulty in school, in traditional male activities, and in friendships. He may start to develop medical problems, such as self-inflicted wounds, or may show symptoms of psychological problems, such as depression, rebellion, or hostility toward others. He may turn to drugs and alcohol to try to numb certain feelings.

Sexually, the abuse robs a boy of the opportunity to have early formative experiences that are self-initiated, self-directed, and self-paced. He is denied the experience of relaxed, safe, sexual exploration with a socially appropriate partner. His initial exposure to sex likely involved lack of control over his genital functioning. He may feel betrayed by his penis because it gets hard, signals arousal, and feels good in the midst of an emotionally painful experience. Thus he may fail psychologically to integrate his penis as a positive part of his body. Sexual activity may become fused with such feelings as disgust and anger as a result of the abuse. As a survivor grows older, he may either withdraw from sex or become overactive sexually in an attempt to free himself of the victim role.

A male survivor who withdraws from sex may be attempting to avoid an activity he defines as undesirable, dangerous, or disgusting. Some survivors may experience this withdrawal as a difficulty in establishing relationships, preferring instead an almost asexual lifestyle. One male survivor was abused by his mother, who slept with him when things were going poorly between her and her husband. The abuse occurred when he was between the ages of five and ten. His mother was usually subtle in her behavior toward him; for example, in one instance she convinced him to come into her room and rub lotion on her legs. On occasion, however, she punished him by locking him in a closet. He could not recall having had intercourse with his mother. In a soft-spoken voice, he shared his feelings about women and relationships:

> I guess I am still sort of afraid of women, sexually I mean. I want to be in a relationship, but it never seems to get very far. Things just don't seem to work out. I think women are scared of me, too. They tell me I get too intense and kind of scare them.
>
> I think I am afraid that I will be like my father. My mother was always telling me that men were just brutes and awful and stuff like

that. So I kind of back off when things get, you know, well—sexual, and I have these fears that I am going to get violent or something.

I don't like to be touched too much. It doesn't feel good unless it is someone I am really interested in. And then I just feel the sex part and not the emotional. It feels like I sort of shut off inside until it is over. I don't have any problems with getting hard. It just kind of feels mechanical and not too satisfying.

I am really picky about who I get with; I mean, I don't have very many sexual experiences. I guess I try to find the perfect one and it just seems like the ones I like are not into it. I think women who are always looking like they want to do it turn me off. Maybe it reminds me of how my mom was sometimes.

I don't worry about being gay, but I think a lot of people think I am because I'm not all macho and everything. That kind of bugs me because it isn't true.

Right now I'm not in any relationship. I miss it some, and there are a couple of women I want to ask out, but it's kind of hard. Sometimes I wonder if I'll ever find the right person out there for me. It seems like it would just be easier to not have any sex to worry about. I'm not very clear about it all.

Sexual withdrawal may also occur within the context of a long-term relationship. Michael is a married, twenty-four-year-old recovering alcoholic who has no children. He was molested by his father, who also molested Michael's sisters. He described his current sexual concerns and his beliefs about sex:

My wife would like it if I had more of a sex drive. I just don't feel like doing it all the time. She has a hard time understanding this, but we are working on it and things are getting better.

She is a lot more experienced than I am, and I guess I feel pretty inadequate, like I'm supposed to know more or something. She complains that I treat her more like a sister than a wife. She's kind of overweight, too, and that doesn't help me get any more turned on. I think I don't encourage her to lose weight because she doesn't feel sexy so much and I don't have to deal with it.

My father never really talked about sex, but it was always there. He would question my sisters about where they were going and who they were seeing. It was like he never trusted us. He would accuse my one sister of being a tramp.

He never bothered me much except a couple of times, and when I got bigger he just left me alone. I sort of knew what was going on with my sisters and I always felt like I should have done something to stop it, but I really didn't have any way to do it. I am still afraid of my father a little.

I think I learned that sex hurt people and made them feel bad. So I don't feel that doing things like that with my wife is going to make her feel good. I am afraid it will be like using her or that she would only do it because she had to or was supposed to or something. It just isn't something you do to someone you love, is what I used to think.

I find I do get turned on sometimes, but it's hard for me to keep it up unless I stay really excited, and once it goes down I usually can't get it up anymore. I think it's pretty frustrating for my wife. I love to cuddle and that's good, but I just don't feel like doing any more than that.

The other reaction to the sexual abuse, that of overactive sex, may involve compulsive, addictive behaviors that offer no long-term sexual relief or security. This hypersexuality, which may stem from a man's desire to prove himself sexually, can end up being self-destructive. For instance, a man who desires intercourse with his wife several times a day may lose her in the process. His hypersexuality may interfere with his ability to remain monogamous in a relationship, may put him at risk for developing sexually transmitted diseases, and may involve him in illegal or socially embarrassing situations. Tragically, these driven types of sexual behaviors may lead a survivor into behaving in sexually abusive ways toward others in an attempt to regain sexual control and power in his life. One adult survivor admitted to incestuous contact with over forty members of his extended family.

Some survivors experience both sexual withdrawal *and* overactivity. The following account was given by a man who had been sexually stimulated by both parents for fourteen years:

My parents inappropriately touched me and French-kissed me. Because of the ambiguous nature of the abuse, I learned that all contact was sexual. I became very reluctant to touch people or be touched by them in ways that were too frank. I couldn't judge what was appropriate. Instead of risking making a mistake, I pulled back.

That sense of not knowing what was appropriate undoubtedly led to my intense and long-term sexual experiences with other boys and an enormous amount of masturbation. I developed into a highly sexual person because I was turned on all the time.

The awful thing about the experience was feeling violated and powerless at the same time. Sometimes I still feel dirty and weak and have trouble letting go. Being that vulnerable sexually brings up the old feelings of violation.

Male incest survivors experience a unique set of sexuality concerns that differ from the concerns of female survivors. In response to the incest, male survivors seem to focus on an inner conflict over their sense of gender identity and sexual orientation. While female survivors can psychologically align with victim traits such as passivity, receptivity, and submissiveness without upsetting their sense of femininity, male survivors may experience these traits as a challenge to their masculinity. Two responses are common: rejecting maleness and flaunting it.

A thirty-one-year-old married survivor who had been repeatedly beaten and sexually taunted throughout his childhood by his older brother—who would frequently poke him in the face with his erect penis—withdrew from male stereotypes. He learned to associate maleness with abusiveness. When asked to share his thoughts on masculinity and gender identity, he said,

I have only recently learned that my being an effeminate man is at least partly due to the way I looked and was treated in childhood. I was given a somewhat female name, I was dressed up as a girl, and I was told I looked girlish. I've often thought that perhaps I wouldn't have been hit or sexually teased if I had been a girl. I've never been good at things men are good at, like sports and working on cars. In the past year or so I have deliberately feminized myself in order to distance myself from other men. I have tried to develop my submissive and passive qualities and have indulged in wearing the colorful, frilly, lacy clothes women wear. I think it has resulted in some confusion in my life, especially in my romance with my wife. I am not so feminine as to want a sex change or to be a homosexual. In fact, the big advantage in my life as a man has been that I seem to be able to enjoy sex more easily than women. I have feminized myself because I don't want to be part of the sex that abuses, rapes, oppresses, manipulates, etc. Most women, if not most people, see men this way. I want to be wanted and desired like men desire women dressed in sexy lingerie. I want to find out what it's like to feel and look sexy. I can't expect my wife or any other woman to feel the same way, though; so I suppose I must put it out of my mind.

The other, seemingly more frequent, social response of male survivors is to adopt behaviors at the other end of a masculinity-femininity continuum. Adolescent survivors often display macho, defensive, and aggressive postures. It's almost as though they are struggling to prove that they are not homosexual by not showing any traits that could be construed as feminine. Many sexually abused boys are drawn to a limited stereotype of men. They may become preoccupied with hypermasculine heroes such as He-Man, Rambo, and Hulk Hogan. Sexual contact may be viewed primarily as a way to gain power and control. This attitude distorts sex and alienates survivors from positive relationships. Real intimacy occurs when neither person feels dominated or controlled by the other. Many male survivors may need to learn ways of both mentally and physically dissolving the relationship they feel exists between their sexual arousal and desire for social power. They may need to expand their definition of manhood.

Incest disclosure may be a particularly difficult challenge for men. Few men have publicly identified themselves as incest victims. As a consequence, there exists little social precedence for male survivors to share the secret of the abuse. Disclosure seems to threaten a boy's masculine identity. He may fear that if he makes such an admission, he will be labeled by others as a submissive victim or a homosexual. Because of this common fear, many professionals believe that present estimates of the frequency of incest involving male victims may represent only a fraction of the actual number of cases. One man exclaimed after hearing a talk about incest: "So what! Most of the men I know are incest survivors!"

In general, male survivors seem to consistently discount or minimize early sexual abuse. "It was no big deal"; "I enjoyed it"; and "Later, I wanted it to happen," are comments often made by male survivors in counseling. It may be difficult for a male survivor to accept the notion that the sexual activity was both abusive and coercive. A survivor who states, "But Dad never forced me . . . " may need to learn that there are other types of force besides aggression and violence. Tricking, threatening, seducing, intimidating, bribing, and sweet-talking are all methods used by sexual offenders. When the offender was an older female, such as a mother, aunt, or big sister, the male survivor may feel he had nothing to complain about. As one man stated, "I guess I was lucky; I got a piece of it early." Men are influenced by our culture to view sex more in terms of whether it was easy or hard to get than whether it was a positive or negative experience.

When a male survivor is able to accept that his seduction was abusive, it signifies a major turning point in therapy.

The type and intensity of sexual repercussions from the incest seem to correspond to such factors as the nature and duration of the abuse, the victim's religious and moral beliefs, the victim's coping skills, and the decisions the victim may have made about himself as a result of the abuse. Early sexual experiences that involved physical force, pain, and indignity may leave a male victim feeling unable to achieve self-confidence, self-respect, or a sense of culturally prescribed male dominance. On the other hand, male victims of seduction and entrapment may have an additional set of issues to contend with, such as feeling extremely guilty, emotionally dependent on a partner, and unable to initiate activity or direct the course of a relationship.

Related to these variations in the nature of the abuse are differences in sexual repercussions that appear to be related primarily to the sex of the offender. Male offenders who abuse young male relatives often suffer from strong feelings of inadequacy and powerlessness. The sexual activity may stem as much from a desire to compensate for these feelings as from a desire to satisfy sexual urges. While some offenders are homosexual, many are heterosexual. It is common for offenders to reduce their inhibitions and impulse control through exposing themselves to child pornography, drugs, and alcohol. They may feel very sexually repressed and act morally rigid in their beliefs. Many male offenders were themselves sexually or physically abused. Some molest children of both sexes.

Incest in which the offender was male often seems to have involved overt physical touching. Fondling, masturbation, oral sex, and anal sex are some of the sexual activities that may have been included. Male victims may misinterpret the sexual stimulation and response they felt during the abuse as meaning that they were genuinely attracted to the *maleness* of the perpetrator. This misinterpretation may foster the mistaken conclusion that they must consequently be homosexual. Male survivors may need to realize that sexual organs do what sensitive body parts are supposed to do—respond to erotic stimulation. Same-sex sexual interaction is normally somewhat arousing to people regardless of their own sexual preferences. While male survivors may think that the molestation defined or caused their sexual orientation, it might be more accurate to assume that the early incestuous experiences increased their awareness of sex in general.

Until more research is done on the relationship of sexual abuse to sexual orientation, the significance of incest in affecting later sexual preference can only be surmised. It does appear that males who have been abused by males have a tendency as adults to relate homosexually more often than do nonabused males.[17] Homosexual activity might be preferred because it was a learned response to stimulation or a reaction to fears of relating to women. Some male survivors who were abused by their fathers might feel that their mothers were to blame for not protecting them, whereas their father just couldn't help himself. They may feel a great deal of anger and distrust toward women.

When the offender is a female, the incest often takes a course of emotional and physical seduction. Mothers who molest their sons often cross over appropriate boundaries subtly and over time. Johnson and Shrier found that female offenders were more likely to repeat the molestation and less likely to use force than male offenders.[18] The physical interaction at first may consist of massage, cuddling, and sleeping in the same bed. Later, touching may develop into genital stimulation, oral sex, intercourse, and orgasm. However, overt sexual activity does not have to take place for the male to have been incestuously victimized. Nonviolent sexual abuse is still coercive, power-based, and uncomfortable. By its nature, it cannot be an act of true loving and caring. Psychological and social damage occur when a female offender hinders a boy's development as an independent, self-confident person.

Female offenders capitalize on the sexual innocence of the male child by arousing in him natural desires to explore sexual sensations. The female offender offers the boy the chance to live out an unconscious boyish desire to be seen as a man, equal to or better than his father. But the actual acting out of this fantasy produces a devastating consequence: the boy fails to separate emotionally from his mother or mother figure. Emotional separation is necessary in order for him to later establish a bond with a mate. The boy who is a victim of a female offender gets put in the strained position of having to compete with males older than himself, instead of being free to experience those males as positive role models.

Sexual activity between a boy and an older female often takes place in a physically tender, sensual manner. In order for the boy to get and maintain an erection, he must feel relaxed or at least somewhat at ease. Because of this, male victims may suffer from extreme guilt and a sense of complicity over their role in the sexual activity. The incestuous activity may impair the learning of important social skills, such as the ability to establish an emotionally satisfying relationship with a partner and to take the lead in physically intimate activity.

The male incest survivor may later feel uncomfortable around women. If this discomfort turns to frustration and resentment, he may react by becoming hostile and abusive toward women or he may choose to engage solely in homosexual relationships. Sometimes the male survivor puts himself down and does not feel worthy of the women he meets. He may doubt his ability to be successful in a relationship, and he may question his ability to maintain an erection that will satisfy a partner. A sixty-five-year-old male survivor shared his sexual history:

My early life was entirely dominated by women. The attitude in my mother's extended family was that women were weak and not to be trusted, while men were to be honored and given extra privileges. I was raised by my mother and by a sister who was three years older and literally led me around by the hand for my first four or five years.

My mother had an inordinate interest in sex. When she and my father were divorced, I was fourteen and my older sister was seventeen. My mother began to drink heavily and to behave seductively whenever she was around men. She competed with my sister for the same young men and on at least one occasion had an affair with one of them. She used to take me with her to parties, where I would watch her get drunk and more and more "seductive." The drinking was repulsive to me, and the seductiveness was at the same time repulsive and attractive.

She often asked me to sleep with her, and sometimes I did so. On one of these occasions, she slowly caressed me until I became hard, and then rubbed against me until I ejaculated. I was terrified and swore never to sleep in her bed again. I remember going into her closet later to look at her nightgown. I had started masturbating at that time but was very naive sexually. A few nights later, she asked me again, and I consented with a great feeling of guilt. From that time on, we had sex fairly frequently.

I didn't have the opportunity to mix with girls in school, so I never learned to treat them like ordinary people—they remained "special" to me. For some reason, I felt I had to protect and cherish them. I knew that boys who teased and tormented girls were more popular than I was with them, and I still treated them all like "little ladies." When I was fourteen I was dating, and essentially followed more mature "courtship" rules of behavior. My older sister and her friends were my models, and I liked older girls better than those my own age.

In college I followed the same pattern. Although I dated young women my own age, I treated them with great respect, and during my four years at college did not engage in sex. Almost immediately after college I entered the army, where women were simply not available. Later, I became engaged to a pleasant young woman — not so much because I wanted to get married but because I couldn't think of any way to avoid proposing that wouldn't hurt her feelings. Still no sex. I realized later that I wasn't ready for marriage, so I broke the engagement by mail. I did do some sexual experimenting with prostitutes, and spent nearly a year in a close relationship with a young woman who wanted to retain her virginity. At that time I was fiercely protective of women and hated the way men were treating them, so I entered into a no-sex contract with my friend.

After that ended, I began dating a divorced woman whom I had met several years earlier. I found myself "forced" to marry her. With my ideas about women, I thought I had no alternative. She was definitely the dominant force. In this first marriage (to a woman who very much resembled my mother) I could perform well only if I entered and finished quickly. She became an alcoholic, and it was a most unhappy thirteen-year marriage.

Soon after the divorce I remarried, this time to an openly sexual woman who did a lot to resolve some of my issues about sex. However, my impotence was still a factor, and after ten years of a basically companionable marriage, I left her because she fell in love with a man — partly (she admitted) because he could satisfy her better.

Then I met an exciting woman and I regained most of my self-respect as a man and learned to treat my impotence as a simple deficit. I learned to compensate for it by skillful lovemaking, and found that I had no trouble finding partners who could appreciate my patience and caring.

Then I met my present wife, who is twenty-two years younger than I am. Surprisingly, we have had a wonderful relationship, and although my impotence has continued and grown worse, to the point that I never get a full erection, our lovemaking is beautiful. At this point I am dealing with the possibility that I will soon lose the ability to ejaculate, which is frightening, but I've been dealing with the general problem for so long that I think I'll get through this crisis as well, with her help. What's really important is that my wife's strength as a woman has given me more strength. She has literally taught me to take care of myself and not to count on her for initiative and strength. Some of this she has "told" me, and some of it has come from her behavior. I have learned to talk back to her. I have learned that I don't have to assume that I'm wrong just because she criticizes me. I have learned to set limits and to ask for what I need.

For years, I told stories about an early romance with an "older woman," almost to the point that I fooled myself. But with my first marriage, I disclosed the story and feel relatively easy about it now.

Male incest survivors are more likely than nonabused males to have such sexual problems as difficulty in achieving or maintaining an erection, rapid ejaculation, difficulty in ejaculating, low sexual desire, and low sexual arousal. In 1985 Johnson and Shrier studied forty male incest survivors and found that 25 percent (compared to 5 percent of a control group) suffered from nonorganic sexual dysfunctions. They believe that the true number of survivors with sexual problems is even higher, since some of their population were still too young to have a full sex life and thus could not experience these problems.[19]

As adults, many male survivors report difficulty in establishing relationships that are both sexually *and* emotionally satisfying. It may be too scary or too reminiscent of the abuse for them to experience emotional vulnerability and sexual arousal at the same time. Male survivors may try to override their emotional selves (something most men are trained to do in our culture) by concentrating solely on their sexual performance and physical functioning. The sexual high may come more from thinking about what they are doing to someone else than from feeling nurtured or pleasured by their partner. Such a mechanical focus leads to emotional distance in the relationship and problems with sexual functioning.

During sexual interactions, male survivors may encounter high levels of performance anxiety. Heterosexual males may worry that these sexual difficulties are indicators of homosexuality. Male survivors may also be troubled by triggers that cause flashbacks to the abuse. One survivor explained:

I had a real problem with impotence in my late teens and early twenties. When I was first with a woman I would get too turned on and then have to stop and calm down in order to get any type of erection. I was very concerned about doing it all right, and sex was always a mixture of excitement, fear, and worry.

As I got into more stable and long-term relationships the problem went away, but I still had a real tendency to view relationships as primarily a sexual thing.

I still have a hang-up about my partner being real clean and smelling fresh. If she smells sweaty or has stale breath, it reminds me of my father's smell and I get real turned off and don't want to be anywhere near her.

I also still hate being in hot stuffy rooms because they remind me of my parents' bedroom, where the abuse happened. I get real strong feelings of panic, anxiety, and rage when I feel too closed in. This happens in my relationships too, when I feel closed in and don't have enough space.

Sexually, I feel kind of frustrated at times. It is what I do to get close to my wife, and yet when I get turned on the feeling part just shuts off. I have a hard time letting go and feeling vulnerable, so sex doesn't really get me as close to her as I want it to. It's like I don't feel safe enough being sexual to share feelings, and yet when I have feelings I react by wanting to express them in a sexual way. It feels like a vicious cycle. I don't ever experience the kind of intimacy I really want.

Another survivor described his erectile problems:

During the latter part of my sexual relationship with my mother, I recall that I would not be able to get a second erection after ejaculating, and she was quite critical of that. Some form of secondary impotence has bothered me ever since. I have always lost erections quickly when in the presence of prostitutes—some sort of over-exitement.

Male survivors of incest can and do overcome the sexual repercussions of the early abuse. They can learn to identify the abuse and acknowledge its consequences in their lives. They can learn to recognize and express their anger and resentment toward the offender. They can experience sexual interactions free of abuse and self-defeating patterns. Male survivors can spend time exploring, by themselves or in male support groups, new definitions of what it means to be a man—definitions that underscore assertiveness, sensitivity, and satisfying sensuality. Sexual problems that resulted from the incest can be resolved. Sex can be an expression of real caring, love, and enjoyment. Male survivors have the right to enjoy positive, healthy sexuality. As one man said:

I feel whole sexually for the first time in my life. I've learned to explore my sexuality without fear and guilt. I feel like there is hope. What I lost as a child I have now begun to reclaim as my own.

Appendix B
Review of Research

I n 1981 Judith Herman interviewed forty women who were in therapy and actively pursuing incest resolution. Fifty-eight percent had never told their mothers or anyone else about the incest while living at home. Fifty-five percent reported sexual problems; 35 percent defined themselves as promiscuous; 45 percent became pregnant during adolescence; 60 percent had had major depressive episodes; 37.5 percent had attempted suicide; and 35 percent had experienced drug or alcohol abuse. Sexual problems included little or no pleasure in sex, flashbacks (memories of the incest intruding in current lovemaking), and pairing arousal so thoroughly with being controlled and dominated that relaxation was impossible. Two of the forty women in the study were lesbians and felt their sexual orientation had been influenced by incest. Three other women defined themselves as bisexual.

One of the most extensively reported studies of incest victims was done by Karin Meiselman in 1978. Working with clinicians at a large Los Angeles mental health clinic, she interviewed the therapists and read the files of fifty-eight clients in therapy over a three-year period. These women were compared to a random sample of one hundred clinic files. She found that 87 percent of her sample had current or previous sexual problems, compared to 20 percent in the control group. Orgasmic problems were found in 74 percent, and 19 percent were promiscuous.

In 1982, Becker, Skinner, Abel and Treacy interviewed eighty-three incest and rape victims about sexual dysfunction since the assault. Fifty-six percent reported at least one sexual problem, with no statistical difference between rape and incest victims in the number of sexual problems experienced. Incest victims who were dysfunctional (N = 12) were more likely than nondysfunctional subjects to have been verbally rather than physically coerced into sex with the perpetrator. Types of sexual problems among dysfunctional incest victims were fear of sex (75 percent), arousal dysfunction (41.7 percent), desire dysfunction (33.3 percent), and lack of orgasm with partners (33.3 percent). Eight percent experienced lack of orgasm in all situations.

In 1979, Tsai, Feldman-Summers and Edgar compared three groups of thirty women each: one clinical (women in therapy for problems associated with childhood molestation), one nonclinical (women molested as children who had never sought therapy and considered themselves well adjusted), and one control (women who had not been molested). The clinical group was found to be significantly less satisfied with their sexual and other relationships with men, were less responsive, had more sexual partners, and had fewer orgasms than women in either of the other groups.

In 1978, Tsai and Wagner studied fifty women who had been molested as children; 97 percent of these had been molested by someone with whom they had had a prior relationship. Three primary areas of sexual dysfunction were identified. Women with these problems were described as nonresponsive, orgasmic without enjoyment, and sexually aroused only when they were in control of the situation. Flashbacks were common for them. The researchers found that these women had a strong need to be affirmed as individuals independent of their sexuality.

Poor sexual-emotional satisfaction was found in a majority of incest-affected women studied by Van Buskirk and Cole in 1983. While most of these women preferred male partners, two thirds had had female sexual partners. The women were said to fear sex and to either withdraw or become promiscuous. The small number of subjects in this study (N = 8) makes the data less tenable than it would be if the study were larger.

Gordy found in 1983 that a "splitting" phenomenon was common among incest-affected women, that is, the women could be *either* sexual or affectionate with a partner but could not combine sex and affection with the *same* partner. She drew the conclusion that the combination brought back memories that were too intense. She also found considerable self-destructive behavior in these women—the use of drugs, suicide attempts, promiscuity, prostitution, and weight loss to the point of eliminating menstrual periods.

McGuire and Wagner found in 1978 that women who had been molested as children had trouble becoming sexually aroused. They found that many of these women were easily orgasmic once the sex act was occurring; however, there was no enjoyment or pleasure in the sexual contact. Gelinas found in 1983 that orgasmic difficulties and difficulty with sexual contact were primary sexual dysfunctions.

In our research we analyzed the responses of thirty-five incest survivors to a questionnaire about their sexuality and its possible relationship to their incest experience. All subjects were currently in therapy for incest concerns. Both arousal and lack of orgasm were problems, but arousal was a more frequent one. The following table lists the sexual concerns identified by women in our study. Our data also indicated that women under age thirty-five had significantly more painful intercourse and felt more concern about the reaction of partners than did women aged thirty-five or older.

Table B–1
Sexual Concerns of Incest Survivors (N = 35)

Issue	% Survivors in Our Study Who Considered This a Problem
Lack of arousal	80
Low arousal	80
Social withdrawal to avoid issue of sex	76
Lack of orgasm with partner	74
Fear of sex	71
Confusion about the normal sequence of dating and sexual behavior	69
Difficulty setting sexual limits	66
Aversion to specific sexual acts experienced during incest	66
Forcing self to have sex	66
Flashbacks to incest during sex	62
Painful intercourse	60
Feelings of sexual power over men	51
Using sex to get attention	48
Worry about partner's reaction to incest	48
Sexual enjoyment only after penetration has occurred	48
Lack of orgasm under any circumstances	46
Physical reactions during sex, e.g., chills	46
Indiscriminate choice of partners	40

Appendix C
Worksheet on a
Sequence of Dating
and Sexual Behaviors

B elow is a list of activities that might describe a typical sequence of dating and sexual behavior for a couple. While there is no "right" sequence, studying this list can help you clarify issues for yourself as you develop a sequence of your own. With several friends, or in a therapy group, you can discuss the sequence in more detail.

talking

participating in group activities

becoming friends

holding hands

touching shoulders, knees, and so forth

spending time together in nonsexual activities

hugging

kissing

petting with clothes on

petting with some clothes off

engaging in genital stimulation

making commitment to relationship and plans for future activities together

engaging in intercourse

Questions:

1. After examining each activity in its given order, explain why this order was chosen. For example, why would kissing come after holding hands? Why might a commitment to the relationship come before intercourse?

2. How long do you think the couple should engage in each activity before moving on to the next one?

3. What danger signals might come up that would indicate it would not be a good idea to proceed to the next step at that time?

4. What could you do if you weren't ready to proceed to the next step but your partner was?

5. What could you do if you moved to the next step but found it uncomfortable?

6. Is the sequence of activities the same for all of your relationships?

7. Do you think a couple is ready to have intercourse if they feel too uncomfortable with each other to discuss birth control?

8. What concerns do you have about relationships, and how can you develop a sequence of activities of your own that will help you address your concerns?

Notes

1. D. Finklehor (July–August 1984), How widespread is child sexual abuse? *Children Today* 3, no. 4: 2.

2. D. Finkelhor (October 1979), What's wrong with sex between adults & children: Ethics & the problem of sexual abuse, *American Journal of Orthopsychiatry* 49, no. 4: 694–695. Reprinted, with permission, from the American Journal of Orthopsychiatry. Copyright 1979 by the American Orthopsychiatric Association, Inc.

3. Sexual Assault Center, Harborview Medical Center (n.d.), *Sexual Abuse: The Mother's Experience,* 2–3.

4. Ibid.

5. Behavior signs and indicators that a child has been sexually abused (October 1983), *Sexuality Today* 6, no. 52: 2. Used with permission of Atcom, Inc., 2315 Broadway, New York 10024.

6. F. Putnam, M.D. (April 1984), New evidence links multiple personalities with sexual abuse, *Sexuality Today* 7, no. 25: 3.

7. D. Gelinas (1983), The persisting negative effects of incest, *Psychiatry* 46, no. 4: 316.

8. D. Finkelhor (1979), *Sexually Victimized Children* (New York: Free Press), 25, 47.

9. Adapted from P. Carnes (1983), *The Sexual Addiction* (Minneapolis, Minn.: CompCare Publications), 97.

10. J. James and J. Meyerding (1978), Early sexual experiences as a factor in prostitution, *Archives of Sexual Behavior* 7: 31–42.

11. National magazine: The dangerous eroticization of children (January 1984), *Sexuality Today* 7, no. 15: 1.

12. R. Johnson and D. Shrier (July 1985), 15, Massive effects on sex life of sex abuse of boys, *Sexuality Today* 8, no. 39: 1–2.

13. D. Gelinas, The persisting negative effects of incest, 326.

14. G. Faria and N. Belohlavek (October 1984), Treating female adult survivors of childhood incest, *Social Casework* 65, no. 8: 468–469. Used with permission of Family Service America.

15. Ibid., 469.

16. L. McGuire and N. Wagner (1978), Sexual dysfunction in women who were molested as children: One response pattern and suggestions for treatment, *Journal of Sex and Marital Therapy* 4: 14.

17. R. Johnson and D. Shrier, Massive effects on sex life of sex abuse of boys, 1.

18. Ibid., 1.

19. Ibid., 1–2.

Bibliography

Becker, J., Skinner, L., Abel, G., and Treacy, E. (1982). Incidence and types of sexual dysfunctions in rape and incest victims. *Journal of Sex and Marital Therapy* 8: 65–74.

Carnes, P. (1983). *The Sexual Addiction* (Minneapolis, Minn.: CompCare Publications).

Faria, G., and Belohlavek, N. (October 1984). Treating female adult survivors of childhood incest. *Social Casework, 65, no. 8:* 465–470.

Finkelhor, D. (1979). *Sexually Victimized Children* (New York: Free Press).

Finkelhor, D. (October 1979). What's wrong with sex between adults and children: Ethics and the problem of sexual abuse. *American Journal of Orthopsychiatry* 49, no. 4: 694–695.

Forward, S., and Buck, C. (1978). *Betrayal of Innocence* (New York: Penguin Books).

Gelinas, D. (1983). The persisting negative effects of incest. *Psychiatry* 46: 312–332.

Gil, E. (1983). *Outgrowing the Pain.* (San Francisco: Launch Press).

Gordy, P. (1983). Group work that supports victims of childhood incest. *Social Casework* 64: 300–307.

Herman, J. (1981). *Father-Daughter Incest* (Cambridge, Mass.: Harvard University Press).

James, J., and Meyerding, J. (1978). Early sexual experiences as a factor in prostitution. *Archives of Sexual Behavior* 7: 31–42.

Johnson, R., and Schrier, D. (15 July 1985). Massive effects on sex life of sex abuse of boys. *Sexuality Today* 8, no. 39: 1.

McGuire, L., and Wagner, N. (1978). Sexual dysfunction in women who were molested as children: One response pattern and suggestions for treatment. *Journal of Sex and Marital Therapy* 4: 11–15.

Meiselman, K. (1978). *Incest: A Psychological Study of Causes and Effects with Treatment Recommendations* (San Francisco: Jossey-Bass).

Putnam, F. (Spring 1985). Pieces of the mind: Recognizing the psychological effects of abuse. *Justice for Children* 1, no. 1.

Sexual Assault Center, Harborview Medical Center, Seattle, Washington. Various handouts.

Tsai, M., Feldman-Summers, S., and Edgar, M. (1979). Childhood molestation: Variables related to differential impacts on psychosexual functioning in adult women. *Journal of Abnormal Psychology* 88: 407–417.

Tsai, M., and Wagner, N. (1978). Therapy groups for women sexually molested as children. *Archives of Sexual Behavior* 7: 417–427.

Van Buskirk, S., and Cole, C. (1983). Characteristics of 8 women seeking therapy for the effects of incest. *Psychotherapy: Theory, Research, and Practice* 20: 503–514.

Woititz, J.G. (1985). *Struggle for Intimacy* (Pompano Beach, Fla.: Health Communications).

Suggested Resources

Outgrowing the Pain, by Eliana Gil, 1983 (San Francisco: Launch Press).
A short, readable book for adult survivors of child abuse which clearly explains how early abuse affects self-esteem and relationships. Especially good for people who wonder whether they were actually abused.

Betrayal of Innocence, by Susan Forward and Craig Buck, 1978 (New York: Penguin Books).
Basic information on the history and dynamics of incest, including many case examples. Sections on variations of incest, including mother-daughter, mother-son, father-son, and sibling.

Father-Daughter Incest, by Judith Herman, 1981 (Cambridge, Mass.: Harvard University Press).
A comprehensive book on how incest affects daughters, including a historical overview, research findings, and treatment concerns.

For Yourself: The Fulfillment of Female Sexuality, by Lonnie Barbach, 1976 (Garden City, New York: Anchor Books).
A good overview of sexual socialization and sexual pleasuring. Especially helpful for women resolving orgasmic difficulties.

For Each Other: Sharing Sexual Intimacy, by Lonnie Barbach, 1982 (New York, New York: New American Library).
Female perspective on healthy couples sexuality. Lots of exercises and suggestions for improving physical relationships. Contains basic sex therapy techniques.

Male Sexuality: A Guide to Sexual Fulfillment, by Bernie Zilbergeld, 1978 (Boston: Little Brown and Company).
Excellent section on male sexual socialization, harmful myths, and reasons for male sexual problems. Includes sex therapy techniques for treating common male dysfunctions.

Out of the Shadows: Understanding Sexual Addiction, by Patrick Carnes, 1983 (Minneapolis, Minn.: Comp-Care Publications).

Overview of common types of sexual addictions, including incest. Can help survivors understand why some perpetrators sexually molest.

Learning About Sex: The Contemporary Guide for Young Adults, by Gary F. Kelly, 1977 (Barron's Educational Series, Inc., 113 Crossways Park Drive, Woodbury, New York 11797).

A good book for teens over fifteen years old and their parents, in paperback. Straightforward sex education for older adolescents. Includes section on love, responsible sex, and decision making in relationships.

"Identifying and Treating the Sexual Repercussions of Incest: A Couples Therapy Approach," by Wendy Maltz, *Journal of Sex & Marital Therapy,* Vol. 14, No. 2, Summer 1988, pp. 142–170.

Primarily written for clinicians. Presents a model for assessing and treating the sexual effects of incest in couple relationships. Includes intervention strategies, techniques, and therapeutic considerations.

Partners in Healing: Couples Overcoming the Sexual Repercussions of Incest (VIDEO) produced by Wendy Maltz, Steve Christiansen and Gerald Joffe, 1988. (For information and to order, contact: Independent Video Services, 401 E. 10th St. Dept. L, Eugene, Oregon 97401, telephone 503–345–3455).

Hosted by Wendy Maltz, this video program helps couples identify sexual problems caused by incest histories, and journey toward sexual healing and emotional intimacy. Symptoms of sexual concerns and specific steps in the healing process are discussed. Features three heterosexual couples (one with a male survivor). Helpful to incest survivors as well as a resource for therapy, education and training.

Two major self-help organizations for adult incest survivors are *VOICES* (Victims of Incest Can Emerge Survivors) in Action, Inc., P.O. Box 148309, Chicago, Illinois 60614, and *ISA* (Incest Survivors Anonymous), P.O. Box 5613, Long Beach, California 90805–0613.

Index

About the Authors

Wendy Maltz, M.S.W., is a registered clinical social worker, a licensed marriage family child counselor, and a certified sex therapist with over eight years' experience treating incest and sexuality concerns. She received a B.A. in psychology from the University of Colorado–Boulder in 1972 and a master's in social welfare from the University of California–Berkeley in 1975. Wendy has worked in a variety of clinical settings, including mental health agencies, schools, and women's centers. Since 1978 she has maintained a private practice in psychotherapy and relationship counseling. In addition to her practice, Wendy has given public and clinical presentations on sexuality topics including seminars on treating the sexual repercussions of incest. She has published several articles and a counselor training manual. Wendy is a member of the Lane County, Oregon, Sex Education and Therapy Consultants and the American Association of Sex Educators, Counselors and Therapists.

Beverly Holman holds an M.S. in counseling psychology from the University of Oregon, where her master's thesis was entitled "The Sexual Impact of Incest on Adult Women." She also holds an M.A. in human development from the University of Kansas. Beverly is currently in private practice in counseling and mediation, specializing in incest and couples counseling. She is also a family therapist at a local agency, where she works with children and adolescents and their families. Previously she counseled in a family-oriented agency, where she led incest groups for adult survivors and worked with abused children and their parents. She is a member of the Oregon Counseling Association, the American Association for Counseling and Development, the Academy of Family Mediators, and the Executive Board of the Family Mediation Association of Lane County, Oregon.